Helen is exactly the kick in the pants I need as a mom. By casting a vision of motherhood that includes little details of family life and the big picture of global injustice and suffering, Helen gives moms the encouragement we need to follow God wherever He might lead us.
—Carla Barnhill, author of *The Myth of the Perfect Mother,* cofounder of themommyrevolution.com

You will be inspired, challenged, and energized [by *The Missional Mom*] to make your home a place of love and service to others. Don't underestimate the power of women, especially the power of a cadre of mothers, who manage their homes as missional outposts for kingdom work.
—Arloa Sutter, executive director, Breakthrough Urban Ministries

The Missional Mom is a treat for any mom who believes that God has called her to serve beyond the reaches of motherhood. Helen shows us how we can at once be wonderful, loving moms while also serving our wonderful, loving God using the vast and divergent passions and gifts He's given us.
—Caryn Dahlstrand Rivadeneira, author of *Mama's Got a Fake I.D.* and cofounder of themommyrevolution.com

Helen Lee is not only a missional mom, she also is a clear and incisive writer. I'm not a mom, but as a Christian and a dad, I found myself marveling and motivated as I read this book. Now this is living!
—Marshall Shelley, editor, *Leadership Journal*

The Missional Mom is a book that challenges us (not just moms!) to embrace radical, countercultural followership especially within the environment of our homes. The wonder years of growing families shouldn't be seen as a time we check out of following God. Helen stirs our imagination to go deeper into who we are called to be in our homes and beyond.
—Dave Gibbons Author of *The Monkey and the Fish: Liquid Leadership for a Third-Culture Church* and *Xealots: Defying the Gravity of Normality*

We are both convinced that in order to unleash the world transforming power of missional Christianity we are going to need to learn a whole lot more from women. We look forward to a time when men and women are released to be all they can be in God for the sake of His kingdom. Helen's book is a wonderful gift to all of us.
—Alan and Debra Hirsch, authors of *Untamed: Reactivating a Missional Form of Discipleship*

There is no sphere of human life that cannot find its true end in God's mission. Helen Lee, with engaging yet powerful prose, helps us see what this might mean for mothers. Under her careful guidance, we see how the rhythms and struggles of being a mom become subsumed by God's sovereign purposes for the redemption of the world. I encourage us all who have families (not just moms) to read this book!

> —David Fitch
> reclaimingthemission.com
> B. R. Lindner Chair Evangelical Theology
> Northern Seminary

It is easy to understand why moms might lose sight of the purpose and meaning for their lives when life is going by at such a frightening speed. This is a book that reminds women of the adventure of missional living (amidst the daily grind) that God is calling all of us to.

> —Michael Wallenmeyer, MissionalinSuburbia.com

This is a serious book, and it will stand out in a landscape littered with feel-good messages for moms. Helen Lee elevates motherhood by challenging us to be more than moms. She affirms our calling, first and foremost, to be God's people.

> —Amy Simpson, vice president, Church Ministry Media
> Group, Christianity Today International,
> editor-in-chief, Kyria.com

I was captivated by the deep spiritual truths in *The Missional Mom.* This book is a wealth of practical and meaningful insight that has everything to do with how to live our lives and raise our children in an increasingly out-of-control culture. Can't wait for The Missional Dad!

> —Tom Davis
> CEO, Children's Hopechest
> Author, *Red Letters, Fields of the Fatherless,* and
> *Scared—A Novel on the Edge of the World*

The Missional Mom removes the pressure of having to always "do" the right thing as a parent and restores a sense of passion and calling to parenting while giving us the right to simply be who it is that God has gifted us to be.

> —Dave Ferguson
> Lead pastor, Community Christian Church
> Movement leader, NewThing

Helen Lee was "missional" before missional was cool—as a journalist, an entrepreneur, a neighbor, wife, and mom. Her life has been defined by service to others and by approaching whatever task that's set before her as a divine calling.

> —Edward Gilbreath
> Editor of UrbanFaith.com
> Author of *Reconciliation Blues*

the
missional
mom

LIVING WITH PURPOSE AT HOME & IN THE WORLD

HELEN LEE

MOODY PUBLISHERS
CHICAGO

© 2011 by
HELEN LEE

Edited by Annette LaPlaca
Interior design: Ragont Design
Cover design: Maralynn Rochat
Cover image: iStock
Author photo: Michael Hudson Photography

Library of Congress Cataloging-in-Publication Data

Lee, Helen, 1976-
   The missional mom : living with purpose at home and in the world /
Helen Lee.
      p. cm.
   Includes bibliographical references (p.   ).
   ISBN 978-0-8024-3786-0
   1. Mothers—Religious life. I. Title.
BV4529.18.L44 2011
248.8'431--dc22

                                                                2010038444

We hope you enjoy this book from Moody Publishers. Our goal is to provide high-quality, thought-provoking books and products that connect truth to your real needs and challenges. For more information on other books and products written and produced from a biblical perspective, go to www.moodypublishers.com or write to:

Moody Publishers
820 N. LaSalle Boulevard
Chicago, IL 60610

3 5 7 9 10 8 6 4 2

Printed in the United States of America

For my three sons
and for Brian, without whom I'd have
neither our boys nor this book.

Contents

INTRODUCTION

What Happened to the Joy of Parenting?

Suddenly, one day, there was this thing called parenting.
Parenting was serious. Parenting was fierce.
Parenting was solemn.
It was active, it was energetic, it was unrelenting.
NORA EPHRON

Last year, I found my ideals about motherhood challenged by an unexpected reality star. Molly the Barn Owl[1] became an Internet sensation when she chose to build her nest in an owl box installed years earlier by a retired couple in San Marcos, California. Unbeknownst to Molly, the box was wired to a videocamera that began broadcasting live feeds of her every move. As she crafted her nest and laid her eggs, she became the most famous barn owl in the world, with nearly ten thousand daily visitors to the 24/7 live feed. Molly (and her eventual offspring) made appearances on numerous media outlets, from local papers to "The Early Show" on CBS; they were celebrities with no idea they were being watched by millions. It was *The Truman Show* and *Animal Planet* all rolled into one, and I was riveted.

After her four owlets hatched, Molly's behavior with her little ones fascinated me. She would gently but firmly walk the line between letting them explore the owl box and sheltering them under the security and warmth of her prodigious wingspan. How naturally and easily it all came to her, a first-time mother with nary a hesitation or uncertainty about how to raise her children. She never complained or got upset; she seemed tired but not overwhelmed. Day after day her owlets grew stronger and bigger, and within four months they were ready to venture into the world on their own. In a single season, Molly had successfully completed a tour of motherhood, just as she was designed to do.

I admit it: I was somewhat envious. Motherhood came so easily to Molly, and there was a part of me that wished it could be as effortless for me. From the moment my first son was born, I was beset with questions. First I confronted the typical questions about newborn care: cloth diapers or disposable? Bottle or not? Was that a gassy cry or a tired cry or a cold cry or a wishing-to-be-back-in-the-womb cry or all of the above? Then came the more insistent, deeper questions, the "who am I, now that I'm a mom?" queries that would come to mind as I stumbled around the hallways with my wide-awake baby boy in the middle of the night or, years later, as I was elbow deep in Lego blocks and Star Wars lightsabers trying to placate my three (fighting) sons.

I wasn't sure what my purpose or place was in life anymore. My questions increased in number and intensity:

- ❂ Was this the life God intended for me?
- ❂ Was losing myself in my home life—leaving behind all semblance of the person I used to be—what motherhood was all about?

- ❂ If motherhood was supposed to be a high and holy calling, why was the daily experience so often draining and joyless?
- ❂ What was I supposed to do with my pre-motherhood experiences and education, with the gifts and talents God had given me, which I never seemed to be using anymore?
- ❂ Was I just not being sacrificial and loving enough to my kids?
- ❂ *Was I a bad mother to be asking these questions?*

But I was not the only mother who asked these kinds of questions. Caryn Rivadeneira, author of *Mama's Got a Fake I.D.*, formerly served as the managing editor of *Christian Parenting Today* magazine. In that role, she discovered that scores of Christian moms wrestled with the same sense of loss and struggle over their identity. Rivadeneira writes, "I realized then that I wasn't a freak of nature. Many of us are in the same boat: The Moms Who Long to Be Known for Who We *Really* Are."[2]

Typical, modern American mothers often feel overwhelmed by these questions of identity and purpose, none of which seem easy. Our mothers and grandmothers came from entirely different societal contexts, so they have not been able to give us the answers we crave. In our grandmothers' generation, women largely assumed they would take their place in a traditional family structure. In our mothers' generation, staying at home seemed a throwback to a bygone era, and "latchkey kids" (I was one) were common. In our generation, we see the full gamut, from full-time working moms to part-time working moms to stay-at-home moms to work-at-home moms, with proponents on the extreme ends of the spectrum so vociferously defending their choices that the phrase "Mommy Wars" has sadly become all-too-familiar.

Yet no one really seems happy about her situation. Carla Barnhill, author of *The Myth of the Perfect Mother*, alerted me to a recent article in *New York* magazine that features the subtitle, "Why Parents Hate Parenting." And in case you're assuming that

Christian moms never think this way, think again; after Barnhill posted the article on the Mommy Revolution blog she writes with Caryn Rivadeneira (www.themommyrevolution.wordpress.com) for an audience of Christian mothers, the first person to comment said, "I just told my husband last week how unhappy I am . . . I'm empty, exhausted, and fried."[3] As I read through the other posted responses, I noticed how many women resonated with the reality that as much as they loved their children, they did not often love the experience of motherhood.

What keeps these women from being able to embrace and enjoy motherhood? What is the source of the conflicts Christian moms are experiencing? Perhaps well-meaning women wrestle with motherhood because they have misunderstood the actual purpose of motherhood. With few exceptions, it is difficult to find books in the world of Christian publishing that address the ambivalence and conflicts Christian mothers experience.[4] I hope to shed light on some of the reasons today's Christian moms encounter despair and difficulty in parenting and provide ideas for positive change.[5]

A few years ago I was given an assignment to write about growing trends in the "missional church" for *Leadership Journal,* a magazine for pastors and church leaders. I hadn't heard much about the term "missional" before then, although the actual word has been around for more than a hundred years. Darrell Guder's book *Missional Church* is credited with renewing interest in the idea that the entire church (as opposed to just the missions committee of a church) should be mission-oriented.[6] And the idea of being missional does not just refer to church but also applies to individual Christians. Alan Hirsch, author of *The Forgotten Ways,* says that a "missional theology . . . applies to the whole life of every believer. Every disciple is to be an agent of the kingdom of God, and every disciple is to carry the mission of God into every sphere of life."[7] The more I spoke with leaders who identified themselves as missional, the more intrigued I became. While there is nothing new about the idea of being missional, as evidenced by the early church, I could see that, two millennia later, our current day churches had largely lost missional urgency.

Then a realization hit me: If the missional movement encouraged *all* believers to adopt a mission-oriented perspective, that included moms. I hadn't heard about Christian mothers who were adopting this perspective, although I was sure they existed. I decided to try to find out if missional moms were experiencing a different kind of motherhood that I might want to emulate. I wanted to learn if living missionally helped them address the questions that continued to vex me and other mothers I knew.

I looked for mothers who lived with God-directed intentionality and purpose, in their family life as well as in whatever other context God had placed them. They were all women who deeply desired to bring change to the world in some tangible way. I spoke with mothers from a diverse range of backgrounds, but as time went by I noticed that a predominantly large segment of the group comprised women who particularly felt called to serve those who are poor. The missional moms I encountered do not make up an exhaustive survey, but these women represent a cross section, a thin slice of the wide range of missional moms in the world today. Their experiences and wisdom provide a glimpse into the multitudinous ways Christian moms today are living out their callings and experiencing a deep sense of joy and fulfillment.

I did not expect how much the experience of interacting with these moms would change my own life. Last year, as a direct result of researching this book, I began homeschooling, which has become a large part of my own journey toward missional living. (You will find out more about this decision in chapter 11.) One of our assignments for the year was to complete a study on birds. My boys and I hung up one feeder and waited to see if anything would show up. One day later, our first black-capped chickadee arrived. Soon a brown-and-white-streaked house sparrow appeared, then a bright yellow goldfinch so vivid I couldn't believe

I'd never noticed it in our yard before. We were hooked. Nine months later, to my husband's bemusement, our backyard housed five kinds of feeders, each with its own type of food to attract a range of twenty bird species, and counting. I used to go outside and just vaguely register the indeterminate sounds of birds; now a whole new world of understanding has opened for me and my family as we have grown in appreciation for the diversity of God's creation.

I hope that by discovering the diversity of missional moms in the following pages, your understanding of motherhood will expand exponentially. My life has been irrevocably changed by spending time with so many inspiring, God-loving women. Their mission-driven lives and commitment to passing their lifestyle on to their children has challenged and humbled me. I hope that seeing this kind of motherhood in action will similarly help you evaluate your own lifestyle and perspectives, so motherhood can become a much more joyful, meaningful, purposeful undertaking.

I also long to see the church gain a newfound appreciation for the diversity that exists among Christian mothers and to affirm and support this diversity. Much in the same way I've learned to appreciate and admire the distinctions among the vast array of birds in our backyard, I have also realized there is no one way to be a "good Christian mom." This book, I hope, celebrates the unique and individual way God has created and called each one of us.

There is no way fully to capture the range and breadth of today's missional moms, but I am glad to offer a start, and I welcome other voices to add to the conversation so we can learn even more from one another. (Visit www.themissionalmom.com for more detailed stories about these women and others not included in this work or share your own stories about being missional as well.)

Women have been the secret weapon in the church since the beginning of its existence, contributing significantly to the progress the church has made in the world. These accomplishments came from ordinary women doing extraordinary things, not out of a desire to bring credit to themselves, but from sincere hearts to serve and love those whom God has called them to serve. The missional moms you will meet in this book take their callings as mothers and wives seriously, but they are also dedicated to furthering God's kingdom. They seek to place God first and foremost, even if it comes at a cost to their families. They live countercultural lives, lives that may look "foolish" in the eyes of the world but that reflect great wisdom in the eyes of the Lord.

Ultimately, mothers who choose a missional lifestyle have found the secret to the conundrum many mothers experience: that living missionally brings a profound sense of heavenly affirmation and peace. As Rivadeneira writes, "We honor God when we honor His creation—women in all their roles, using all their gifts God gave them."[8]

Most American mothers—who have the means to purchase a book and the education to read it—are among the richest people on the planet, educationally and materially. The Bible says in the book of Luke, "From everyone who has been given much, much will be demanded." We have the privilege and blessing to be able to ponder questions of calling, priorities, and lifestyle, and those of us who have been given this opportunity must not take it lightly. On behalf of a hurting, fallen world that needs as many as are willing to wholly embrace God's call, will you heed that call? My hope is that you will find guidance, direction, and inspiration to join those already gladly and fully embracing the life journey of the missional mom.

CHAPTER ONE

The Missional Mom
Embraces the Call of
Her Missional God

God's call is often demanding.
It will require sacrifice of some kind,
and possibly some hardship.
But it will result in meaning and purpose.
You can be sure of that.

OS GUINNESS

I confess I always had a hankering for musically gifted men. I fell for my future husband when I attended his junior-year recital in college and heard him thunder away at the Brahms Piano Sonata No. 3 with both precision and flair. Fast-forward fifteen years and three kids, and you can probably picture the environment in our house of music lovers. Our boys have been surrounded since before birth by the sounds of everything from Liszt to Motown to Van Halen. And now our kids are at an age to make their own music as budding instrumentalists. One day I was trying to help one of our sons with his new violin piece, a short concerto by Arcangelo Corelli. For the first time, his part was more of a supportive role and did not carry the main melody line. Having been used to a long list of easily hummable children's Suzuki songs, my son was stymied by this piece with no easily recognizable melody. He tried in vain to practice, but I could tell his interest was flagging and his frustration was mounting as he repeatedly fumed, "I just don't get it!"

Thankfully, we had the DVD of his violin school's previous year's concert, and together we watched a performance of the piece he was struggling with. I could see, almost instantly, the difference hearing the whole concerto made. When my son heard the entire song and saw the groups of children playing their distinct parts, some of which he hadn't even known existed, he was able to understand how his particular part fit with theirs. Listening to the performance gave him the full picture of what the concerto would ultimately sound like, and he was much more motivated to work on his part as a result. Before that, just uttering the words "Corelli concerto" would stress out my son. Today, this former nemesis has become a source of joy for him.

We all need to see the big picture of how what we are doing matters. When we don't understand how our efforts make a difference in a tangible way, we can become frustrated and anxious. God has given each human being a purpose and calling in life, and so it is natural to want to know our lives matter in the grand scheme. One of the cruel punishments Nazi soldiers inflicted on imprisoned Jews was to sentence them to forced labor with no discernible purpose or outcome, such as hauling heavy rocks back and forth all day.[1] The punishment was less physical than it was mental.

The same principle operates for us: the more we feel as though our actions and labors are irrelevant, the more despairing and hopeless we can become. As in the *New York* magazine article "All Joy and No Fun: Why Parents Hate Parenting," today's mothers can often reflect that sense of purposelessness and despair in their lives.

Why aren't today's women, Christian or otherwise, discovering more joy and fulfillment in their journey as mothers? Perhaps we have a hard time when we don't understand our life calling and how our contributions make a difference in the larger picture of what God is doing in the world. Perhaps we need to see that bigger picture, just as my son needed to hear the whole concerto, so we can press forward with hope, excitement, and conviction. God has given each of us a piece to play, a melody to fit into the overall redemptive symphony He is writing in the world today. Our job is to discern what our piece is and then to play it with as much skill and passion as we can muster.

So moms need to explore the idea of calling and understand both the specific part God has given them and also how the melody of motherhood fits into the grand symphony of God's work. And as you'll soon see, the life God is intending for you may be different from what you imagine a Christian mother's calling is supposed to be.

THE CHRISTIAN CALLING

To talk about calling, we must start from the beginning and delve into question of calling for every Christian. Each and every person who is a follower of Jesus shares the same calling, which at the core is not something to do but a Person to know: our calling as children of God is to know Him, first and foremost. As Os Guinness writes, "It's not about you. It's about the One who calls you."[2] Our primary calling is to be with God, to immerse ourselves in His immeasurable love and grace. Everything else flows out of this connection, which is our absolute number one priority.

Christians can accept and gloss over this concept too quickly. Moms, in particular, are busy, busy people; we just assume that being with God is a reality in our lives. But give the idea another look: *Our primary calling is to be with God.* The most important word in that sentence is "with," something I learned anew thanks to a recent sermon I heard by Skye Jethani, managing editor of *Leadership Journal.* Jethani said, "Our central calling is to be *with* God, not to do things *for* God," which he feels is a misconception evangelical Christians often hold. He tells the following story about his experiences working with Wheaton College students as they asked questions about the topic of calling:

> I've been doing a ministry with a group of Wheaton College students, and they're great students, great kids . . . But they've had it drilled in them that they are the cream of the crop, the most educated and resourced Christians in the world. So when they come close to graduation, they start flipping out on me. They ask, "What path do I take? I want to go be in that place where I will experience fullness of the Christian calling." They're so consumed with what's on the horizon that they forget they're called to live with Christ right where they are.[3]

It can be easy for all Christians to start thinking that there are things we must "do" for God in order to live more missionally, and I will in fact offer many suggestions along these lines. But the goal of doing things *for* God is a dangerous one unless we place it in proper context. The primary calling for Christians is to be *with* God, in whatever circumstances He has placed us. As we reside in those circumstances with Him, it becomes clearer how we are to serve God in those circumstances. Doing things for God becomes an outflow of our connectedness *with* Him.

As an example, Jethani discusses the scene in Act 16 in which the apostle Paul and his companion Silas were arrested and thrown into prison after being severely beaten. Paul and Silas were "pray-

The Missional Mom

ing and singing hymns to God." They were in the Lord's presence, very much *with* God, so much so that when the earthquake came, their chains were loosened, and the prison doors fell down, Paul and Silas did not choose to escape but remained. Their example of being with God in such a connected way moved the heart of the jailer, who then brought Paul and Silas to his house. Their encounter resulted in the baptism of the guard and everyone else in the household. An entire family was saved due to Paul and Silas's connection with God, despite the difficult circumstances they were in. They never forgot their main calling, to be with God, which subsequently had an impact on the lives around them.

Being *with* God constitutes the first part of the primary calling God has for all Christ-followers. The second part of that call flows naturally from the first, expressed in the Great Commandments Jesus gives in Matthew 22:37–40: "'Love the Lord your God with all your heart and with all your soul and with all your mind.' This is the first and greatest commandment. And the second is like it: 'Love your neighbor as yourself.' All the Law and the Prophets hang on these two commandments." As we remain *with* God, as we love Him with all our heart, soul, and mind, He leads us to the second part of the calling. The apostle John also addresses this Christian call to love God and love our neighbors: "We love because He first loved us," John writes. "If anyone says 'I love God,' yet hates his brother, he is a liar . . . Whoever loves God must also love his brother" (1 John 4:19–21). Loving others is not something we do out of obligation but as a natural response to the love that God has shown for us.

A simple but memorable illustration regarding loving others has stuck with me for decades. I call it the "cup analogy." As God fills our cup with His love, it overflows and spills out from us onto others. Loving our neighbors is the natural outpouring that results from being with God as we pursue Him as our central calling.

While the Great Commandments describe our ultimate calling, the Great Commission as stated in Matthew 28:19, in combination with Jesus' final instructions in Acts 1:8, tells us *how* we are to live out this calling. Jesus gives us our mission, which is twofold:

- ❂ "Be my witnesses in Jerusalem, and in all Judea and Samaria, and to the ends of the earth" (Acts 1:8).
- ❂ "Go and make disciples of all nations, baptizing them in the name of the Father and of the Son and of the Holy Spirit, and teaching them to obey everything I have commanded you" (Matthew 28:19–20).

This twofold mission reflects what God wants to do in and through His people. Throughout history, God has shown Himself to be proactive. He creates the world out of nothing; He fashions humankind out of His own image, and then, when clearly His people need a Savior, God sends His own Son to be the solution. Our God is by no means a passive God, who stays far removed from His creation. What has changed since He sent Jesus, however, are His methods. Now He intervenes in the world through His people, embodied in the church and empowered by His Holy Spirit, as we act as His hands and feet in a fallen and broken world. God's end goal is clear: the redemption of all of creation, as we see depicted in Revelation. But God's methods now involve inviting Christ-followers to participate with Him to bring His love, hope, and healing to those who need it. Through Jesus, God has shown us how He has taken the initiative in the lives of all humanity and also how we are to take the initiative in the lives of the people around us.

So our God is a God on a mission. He is on a mission to redeem all of Creation; our God is a *missional* God. In what seems like an incredible plan, He invites us to partner with Him in this mission. Despite our flaws, despite our weaknesses—or perhaps more accurately, *because* of our flaws and because of our weaknesses—we are called to bear witness to what Christ has done for us and bring that Good News to anyone and everyone, making disciples. As God has been missional in reaching out to us, so must we be missional in reaching out to others. Every one of us is, in fact, a missionary sent by God, loved and empowered by Him to do His will.

Missionaries are not just specially selected people who spread the gospel in distant lands. *You* are a missionary, in whatever context God has placed you, with whatever gifts He has given you. Your mission is to be His witness and disciple-maker wherever you live and move and have your being. This mission does not change when you become a mother.

THE BIG DISCONNECT

On the one hand, it's absolutely and necessarily true that once children come into our home, our lives change dramatically. We have to spend most of our waking (and many of our sleeping!) hours caring for our children, who arrive completely or largely dependent on their parents for all of their basic needs. But, although the circumstances of our lives change when we become parents, our calling remains the same. We are still primarily called to know and love God, then love our neighbors as an outflow of that relationship. Our mission remains to "bear witness" and "make disciples," both activities requiring our continuing participation in the world. The calling and mission God has for us *remains unchanged* once we become wives and mothers.

What I have seen time and time again, in my friends' lives, in my own life, and in the lives of countless others reflected in the Christian and secular media, is that we mothers often forget how motherhood intersects with the bigger picture of our primary calling and mission. Sometimes we replace our primary calling and mission by saying, "Motherhood is my highest calling" or "Motherhood is my primary mission." When a secondary call displaces a primary one, the confusion begins.

Secondary calls, as Os Guinness explains, are the specific ways we live out the primary call to love and know God. Secondary calls vary from person to person; one woman is called to homemaking, for example, while another is called to law or teaching or medicine or a whole host of other options. But, as Guinness writes, "these and other things are always the secondary, never the primary calling. They are 'callings' rather than the 'calling' . . . secondary callings matter but only because the primary calling matters most."[4]

Our lives are full of secondary callings, and being a mother is just one of those secondary callings. In addition to being a mother, I am a wife; I am a daughter; I am a sister; I am a friend; I am an aunt. I am a writer, a member of my church's mercy and justice ministry, a homeschooling parent. If you make a list, your secondary callings will likely look different from mine. We each have an individual set of secondary callings, some of which change over time. Motherhood certainly does not look the same when our children are young compared with when they are in college or beyond. In various seasons of our lives, we may only focus on a few of these callings, and other times we'll focus on others. But none of these secondary callings are more important than the unchanging primary calling—not even motherhood.

I do not mean to devalue motherhood in the least. Motherhood is a critical secondary calling for those of us who have been given the privilege of playing that role in a child's life. But we always need to put our role as mothers in the right context and never prioritize our secondary calling as a mother over our primary calling to know and love God.

God's mission gives us the direction we need to live our lives with the right priority. Motherhood does not provide us with the direction we need to go. If it did, I doubt we would see the proliferation of articles and books about the hardships of motherhood that flood the market today. On the contrary, making motherhood your primary mission could potentially backfire and give your children the wrong message about what our essential life priority is meant to be. But God's mission informs and guides us in all the secondary callings of our lives—motherhood, vocational paths, or our relational roles. As we pursue God's mission in our lives—bearing witness to what Christ has done for us, making disciples here and around the world—we are able to see how He can use our secondary callings as channels through which His primary mission will be accomplished.

What this means is that every role, every job, every activity, every person you encounter presents an opportunity to live out God's primary mission for you, to bear witness to what Christ has done and to make disciples. Whether you are in a vocational setting, a school volunteer committee, at the grocery store or school music rehearsal, or a neighborhood playgroup, you have the chance to do God's work—in other words, to be missional. Sometimes, we get stuck trying to figure out what we are supposed to do with our lives, when all we have to do is pursue God's mission with intentionality right where we already are.

YOUR HOME AS A MISSIONAL OUTPOST

How then should we think about motherhood? One way to adopt a missional perspective is to think of as our homes as "missional outposts." Home is a place where you are nurturing and training the next generation of missional Christians, who will ultimately pursue God's purposes in their own lives. It's the place to give you inspiration and direction, as you seek with your family to discover how God wants to use each of you in His grand mission. Rodney Clapp, author of *Families at the Crossroads*, says that "Christians in our society must retrain themselves to see faith as no less public than private. . . . In a real sense, and like the homes of the New Testament church, our houses must go public. Our call is to live not in private havens or retreats, but in mission bases."[5]

So our goal as mothers is not to invest in family life as an end unto itself. That would be like my son pouring effort into his solitary part and isolating himself from the rest of the orchestra. Instead, we invest in our children to help them see the big picture, the greater purpose to which God is calling our sons and daughters. We strive to train our children with the purpose of preparing them to accept their own calling to be God's missionaries in whatever way He intends. That is missional motherhood. It's about helping your children recognize and play their God-composed songs and to understand how they are participating in the larger symphony He is conducting today.

Let's go back to my son, the violinist. When I help him learn his scales and pieces, my goal is not for him to become an excellent violinist for his own glory—and not even for him to get into a good college one day. My object is to help him develop a talent and a gift to be used for God's purposes. I tell him that the reason we practice is so we keep investing in our gifts as the Bible calls us to do, so that God can use our talents to serve and love others. I am training him to be a missionary in whatever way God intends—and these opportunities can come fairly early in your child's life if you encourage them.

When you see your home as a missional outpost, your role as a mother becomess clearer: to prepare and release the people inside for a lifetime of participating in God's mission to the world. But it also means the family as a whole supports the parents in their respective mission fields. If God has given you a talent or gift in a particular area, find ways to continue developing those gifts and interests to serve His purposes.

I have a friend, Irene Cho, who recently discovered she loves to sew. When she had her two daughters, she put her creative gifts aside because it seemed there just wasn't time for them. Mothers rarely feel there is enough time to invest in whatever creative gifts and talents they might have used before they had

The Missional Mom

children. But we have to proactively *make* time to stay connected with those areas of giftedness, which helps restore our sense of sanity and purpose, as well as teaching children what it means to keep investing in one's talents for God's purposes. Once Irene understood that she needed to invest in her passion for sewing, she began taking classes and sewing at night while the kids were asleep. She creates beautiful handmade bags and clothing, which she gives away to people as her personal ministry of service. Each creation is her labor of love intended to bless others, and Irene now receives an enormous sense of fulfillment and joy. "It's been a wonderful outlet," Irene says. "And I love being able to surprise others with the gift of something personal and handmade."

Using God-given gifts to bring happiness into the life of another? I call that missional living! And as mothers demonstrate this lifestyle, their children learn that their lives are supposed to be about something bigger and better than themselves. They also learn the important lesson that children are not the center of a mom's life, but that moms, too, are colaborers in God's mission, the primary purpose that can give their lives true and lasting meaning.

Seeing the home as the family's mission base also gives mothers a better perspective on the activities and tasks that go on inside their homes. Each household activity can serve as an important channel for fulfilling the mission God has given us. Even the most mundane task—changing a diaper, doing laundry, cleaning the bathroom—can be seen as having eternal value. Any activity that contributes to the larger mission of supporting the "missionaries" in your family can be a sacred act as you undertake the activity *with* God to advance your family's God-given mission. When motherhood becomes missional, we see much more clearly how our actions and activities play a part in God's redemptive work in our fallen world.

We all share the same calling as Christians. We now also understand the shared Christian mission and the overarching purpose of motherhood. But at this point, we shift from the shared purposes to the fun part: how will your motherhood journey and the "missional outpost" you create be unique? No two families are alike, and so there will be great diversity in the ways that missional moms (and dads, too, in two-parent homes) create missional outposts. As a starting point, I offer some pointers to remember as you shape your family's missional culture.

Maximize shared interests for missional purposes. My family is a musical one; your family will have its own strengths and gifts. The qualities that make your family unique will provide the best clues for how you might be missional together. What are the shared interests that can serve as a missional platform for your family?

Melinda Boyle lives in Columbia, South Carolina. She is married, with four children ten years old and younger. Melinda is currently a church interpreter for the deaf in her local community. As her children watched their mom communicate in this way over the years, they began to pick up the skill of using sign language in their own communication with deaf children or adults. "My children have become interested in the deaf and in their lives, and how they have overcome and live with what is called a 'disability,'" Melinda says. "For my kids, it's a way of life now." Melinda's heart and passion for reaching the deaf community—"only 2–4 percent of people who are deaf in America attend church, making them the largest unreached people group in the United States"—have had an impact on her children, who have adopted this missional perspective in their own interactions with the deaf.

Keep pointing your kids toward the primary calling. As I put the finishing touches on this book, my family was more than five hundred miles away, staying with my husband and in-laws so I could complete the project. At first, my kids had a hard time accepting that they would be without Mom for a couple of weeks. I'd never spent this much time apart from my children before! But I repeatedly explained, "Mommy has a job from God to do. I am using my gifts for Him. We must all say 'yes' when God calls us to do something." They came to understand that my priority has to be doing God's work, even if it makes life temporarily difficult for them. And I loved seeing how they came to support my efforts. My older boys prayed for me over the phone every day of our separation, that God would help me and that the book would serve His will. No matter how hard this finite period was on me, my husband, or the boys, they have learned such a valuable lesson in the end: God uses our gifts for His purposes, and when He calls, we must follow.

Remind yourself often of the "big picture" of what God is doing. Last year, one of my sons and I were involved in a car accident. We were driving down a neighborhood street when were were blindsided by a car driven by an eighty-seven-year-old who had missed his stop sign. The impact of our cars sent our minivan into another car waiting in the middle of the intersection. Our minivan was crushed beyond recognition or repair, the groceries I had just bought were smashed and smeared all over our trunk, yet miraculously no one was seriously injured.

The incident was my first real experience with a major automobile collision. I found it amazing how suddenly and quickly life could throw me unexpected curveballs. I appreciated that no one was hurt, but the experience reminded me how fleeting life can be and how any number of factors could have turned a bad situation much, much worse. Life is short. The older I get, the faster it goes. Perhaps this is a sign of a midlife crisis, but I've realized that I always want to keep the end goal in mind, never losing sight of my life's overriding purpose. I don't want to get so mired in—and frustrated by—playing my own little tune that I forget there is a much larger symphony going on around me.

Motherhood can be draining, exhausting, and even stifling at times. We all have those days when our patience is short, our nerves are frayed, and our children drive us bananas! But as we seek to shape our homes into missional outposts, we may discover that motherhood can be as much of an adventure as going to a faraway land as a missionary. And as every missionary has learned, an important step before engaging in missional activity is to understand the cultural context she is ministering in. Mothers here in America need to recognize that our cultural context sends powerful messages that often create barriers in our lives, preventing us from serving God's mission and purpose to the best of our ability. We'll take a look at these barriers in the following chapter.

CHAPTER TWO

The Missional Mom
Resists Cultural
Pressures

*I found out the hard way that
if we don't disciple people,
the culture sure will.*

ALAN HIRSCH[1]

My friend Linda told me a fascinating story about her first day of school as a new graduate student on the campus of a Christian college. The first class she attended was a joint one with undergraduates on the topic of marriage and family, and she arrived wearing a worn sweatshirt and jeans, the standard outfit typical of the secular college in New England she had attended as an undergrad. "I didn't pay much attention to how I looked because it was an 8 a.m. class, and I assumed the rest of the students would have thought and done the same," she said.

Imagine her surprise when she entered the classroom, largely made up of women, and discovered that most of her classmates were already dressed to the nines at that hour. All she could see were beautifully made-up faces and perfectly coiffed hair. There was not another sweatshirt in sight! She tried to cower her way to the back, self-conscious about how ratty she appeared in comparison. "It hadn't even occurred to me that what I thought was standard practice was in fact not the case at a different school!" Linda said, laughing.

Linda had stumbled into a completely different cultural context from what she had known in a campus setting. Although she much preferred her previous college's more casual norms, over time she found herself changing her behavior to more closely match her new cultural context. The sweatshirts moved to the back of her closet, and she started building in more time to get ready in the morning. In the end, the new cultural context swayed her.

Our lives reflect the cultural values we hold. The fact that I am American, married to a Canadian, a Christian, a woman, and a midwesterner, for example, all have impact on the way I live and what I believe about the world, because each one of those traits represents a cultural influence. And missional moms have to fine-tune their sensitivity to cultural forces because being missional is often about doing the very opposite of what the culture around us encourages us to do.

Culture is one of those challenging, slippery words, defined by numerous people in different ways. We'll eventually cover what it means to be a "culture-maker,"[2] but for now we'll explore culture's effects on *how we make sense of the world*. In the classic 1980s movie *The Gods Must Be Crazy*, a random object drops from a plane into the Kalahari desert, where it is discovered by a bushman named Xi. He takes the strange item back to his village, where it causes havoc as people begin to fight over it and even use it as a weapon. Xi concludes that the object is evil and must be taken to the ends of the earth to be destroyed. What was this mysterious, evil-infused object that needed to be removed as far from the village as possible? An empty, glass Coca-Cola bottle. This object, so familiar to those of us in the U.S. and to many around the world, was completely foreign to Xi and his fellow tribe members. His cultural context provided no help for understanding what on earth the mystery object was, whereas you and I, who live in a country in which Coca-Cola is as ubiquitous as water, know exactly what that glass bottle represents.

Most of the time, we are not even aware that we are absorbing understanding, beliefs, and values from the culture. In the same way people who spend a good amount of time in sunny climates develop a perpetual tan without even trying, the longer we are in a particular cultural context, the more likely we are to absorb its rays and become altered by it. No one has ever sat you down in a classroom and taught you that the Coca-Cola logo represents a certain brand or a certain soft drink. You likely can recognize the shape of a Coke bottle and know what it tastes like (and if you have particularly discriminating taste buds, you know the differences among the regular product and the Diet product and the Coke One product or you prefer Pepsi instead). Opinions and information are stored in your head without your having intentionally studied or placed the information there. In both small and significant ways, our cultural contexts shape us each and every day.

For Christians, the danger comes when we begin to blindly accept all of our cultural influences as right and good without contrasting them against God's ideal for us. If I do not take the time to understand cultural influences, then it will be far too easy for me to adopt practices and lifestyles at variance with God's intentions and plans for me. James writes that "friendship with the world is hatred toward God"; these are direct and frank words that we have to consider seriously (James 4:4). We develop friendship with the world as we adopt and follow cultural values that run counter to what God has designed for us, which often happens without our realizing it.

In contrast, missional moms are cognizant of cultural influences, and they make intentional choices to leave behind values that oppose God's design for their lives and the lives of their families. Just as Xi from *The Gods Must Be Crazy* protected his family from a consumer product widely embraced by the rest of the world, missional moms take the time to examine the cultural values around them and turn away from those influences that run counter to Scripture's mandates, no matter how "crazy" it may seem to others.

AMERICA, THE LAND OF THE ACHIEVER

As I was driving along a busy Chicago highway the other day, I saw a simple but striking new billboard sponsored by PNC Bank, yet another entrant in the ever-changing banking market. The large letters of white text stood out on the blue background and read: "For the Achiever in Us All." The statement is meant to be inspiring, but to me it reflected a clear example of how much American culture celebrates achievement. The reason Americans highly value achievement is simple: most believe achievement leads to contentment.[3]

But does achievement really lead to contentment, particularly in the lives of our children? A fascinating recent book by *New York Times* bestselling author Alexandra Robbins entitled *The Overachievers: The Secret Lives of Driven Kids* actually debunks this myth. Robbins followed the lives of a number of high school juniors and seniors who attended Walt Whitman High School (WWHS) in Bethesda, Maryland, considered one of the top public schools in the country.[4] Robbins set out to explore what motivated the students and their parents to be so driven, and what the results were. Her conclusion was not encouraging for those who believe that achievement is the way to contentment: "Over-achiever culture . . . has become a way of life . . . When teenagers inevitably look at themselves through the prism of our over-achiever culture, they often come to the conclusion that no matter how much they achieve, it will never be enough. And the pressure steadily mounts."[5]

Part of the reason I found this book so fascinating is that I, too, am a graduate of Walt Whitman High School. As I read Robbins's book and got to know the students who were similarly scratching and clawing for a place in an ultracompetitive context, I found myself reliving the stress and chaos of my high school days. Of the approximately five hundred students in my graduating class, prob-ably half applied to the same ten to twelve competitive colleges. It's pretty daunting to be forced to see your friends as foes in your quest to achieve the assumed next step in your life progression, meaning acceptance to a (preferably prestigious) college or uni-versity. I found the pressure cooker of Whitman relentless and intense, unhealthy and negative for my own sense of self in many ways. And yet, when it came time for our family to choose a hometown, I discovered I had not learned any lessons from my past.

Naperville is a large suburb about thirty miles southwest of Chicago. Naperville seems on the surface like an ideal community for any family. In 2008 it was rated #3 on *Money* magazine's list of the Best Places to Live due to its strong schools and excellent community resources, including a library system considered the best in the nation for similar-sized cities. When my husband and I moved to Chicagoland, we ultimately chose Naperville for two main reasons. First, there was a critical mass of people from our church who already lived in this city. The second reason was those aforementioned school systems. What I did not recognize at the time of our move was how much I had absorbed the cultural values I had grown up with. Getting the best education you can get was a huge value for my family. The narrative I heard time and time again as a child and teen was to "do well in school so you can go to a good college so you can get a good job and live a good life."

Yet despite the fact that I know full well the pressures of attending a school where achievement is encouraged and over-achievement is celebrated, despite the fact that decades later I can still clearly recall how difficult it felt to be in that kind of environment, despite the fact that I cared less about learning than I did about getting the right grades, *I still ended up making a similar choice for my kids.* The cultural forces that had surrounded me all my life had not lost their hold on me. Without even realizing it, I had bought into a philosophy that placed a high value on academic achievement in order to achieve maximum happiness.

WHO'S IN CONTROL?

This is the achievement-oriented culture that drives so many Americans today. Success is tied to achievement; achievement is evidenced by acceptance to a great college. So a child must be properly nurtured and prepared, starting from the earliest years to guarantee his or her future happiness, and the parents (especially the moms) bear the burden of making such success a reality. Moms are constantly bombarded with the message "You must not fail in your mission to prepare your children to the best of their ability; otherwise they will suffer the consequences!" Many of us feel this pressure and accept this value wholeheartedly—and we are utterly misguided when we do.

"We have adopted our culture's beliefs that we are the primary shapers of our children and that we have control over who they are and who they will become," writes Leslie Leyland Fields in her recent book *Parenting Is Your Highest Calling: And Eight Other Myths that Trap Us in Worry and Guilt.* "This [misconception] reflects our sinful bent to see ourselves as more essential and more in control than we actually are."[6]

Christian mothers who are unaware they are being shaped by the achievement orientation of American culture may well be taking the lives of their children into their own hands, instead of being the shepherds that God intends. How freeing it would be if we could remember that we are *not* the ones in control of our children's future and that God Himself is the one and only Author of our children's tomorrows. How much more peace we would feel if we could take to heart Scripture's admonition not to worry about the future instead of following the false gospel that achievement equals success equals contentment. And how much more our children would enjoy childhood if we released them from an expectation to excel or accomplish for their own future glory.

As our children's first and primary spiritual leaders, our job is to help them understand the difference between succeeding in the world's eyes and living lives worthy of God's calling. The Lord cares less about the achievements and accomplishments of our children than we do. The words we need to repeat to ourselves and our children are not "Be Successful," but "Remain in Him" or "Remain *with* Him."

When we push our children to excel and achieve as their primary goal, when we communicate that their value comes from what they accomplish, we set our children up to swallow a dangerous fallacy: that God loves them for what they do and not for who they are. We also run the risk of a prideful pursuit in which we erroneously believe we can shape their future in ways the world considers most fulfilling and rewarding. But missional moms stand against this cultural fallacy and challenge others to stand against it as well.

Sue Ferguson is on the ministry staff of Community Christian Church (CCC) in Naperville, a city where I've heard mothers lament that if their children don't start organized sports by age four, they will already be behind. Sue is the mother of three children thirteen years old and older. Through her ministry at CCC, she has interacted with numerous moms experiencing the stresses of an achievement-oriented culture. "Some of my friends get very stressed out about what college their child is going to go to. I'm always telling them 'God has a plan for their life and it's not dependent on getting into a certain college,'" Sue says. "My faith that God has a plan for them has taken some of the pressure off. Some parents think their children's whole future depends on which college they go to."

Cyd Holsclaw is another mom introduced to me by missional author and pastor David Fitch, who serves with Cyd at Life on the Vine church in Long Grove, Illinois. Part of what shaped Cyd's anti-achievement cultural outlook was work that she did in an elder-hostel with older adults. "I would ask them what they prized most about their life, what they wished they had done when they were thirty," Cyd says. "One woman was sixty-two, and all her children had no interest in God and the church. She said to me, 'I think about how much time I spent trying to help them be successful, and now I know that true success is not where the world wants us to be.' I have not forgotten those words."

THE CASE AGAINST OVERPARENTING

The relentless drive for success, which Robbins found did not merely reside with the students of a top public high school but all over the country, has manifested itself in a recent cultural phenomenon called "helicopter parenting." Not only do parents "swoop in to solve or prevent their [children's] problems," but they are also "obsessed with their children's statistical achievement and with doing all they can to make sure their children end up at the top."[7]

Particularly among middle- to upper-class families, the extraordinary efforts that moms (and dads) undertake to give their children every opportunity for enrichment and success are so prevalent that *New York Times* columnist Judith Warner captured the frenzy in the title of her 2005 work *Perfect Madness: Motherhood in the Age of Anxiety*. Mothers in this book were depicted as despairing when, for example, their toddlers did not

The Missional Mom

get into the right preschool. *Time* magazine ran a cover story last year called "The Case Against Overparenting: Why Mom and Dad need to cut the strings," detailing how this trend has become increasingly evident in American culture.[8] Christian families have not been immune to these same pressures of emphasizing family life and children to an extreme. Pastor Ed Young writes in his book *Kid CEO* that "parents think they need to give their children undivided attention 24/7. But we need to realize it is possible to give our kids too much attention . . . too much of a good thing can suffocate them.[9]

Helicopter parenting is naturally related to the busyness in today's families, with overpacked schedules full of activities for every child to ensure they build skills and talents early enough in life. Music lessons, sports practices, art classes, tutoring sessions, service opportunities, Bible clubs . . . the list goes on and on. I would even venture to guess that this relentless and increasing busyness is part of the reason we mothers have trouble with motherhood in our day and age.

Of course it's a privilege and a blessing for children to have the opportunity to grow their skills and develop God-given talents. But the question to ask ourselves is this: what is our motivation for involving our kids in all of these activities? Is it so that we can hone them on the achievement-oriented grindstone to increase their chances of ultimate happiness as defined by American culture? Might children be so overbooked with activities that they lose some of the wonder and freedom of childhood, a special time that only comes around once?

The busyness problem is so pervasive that in 2007 the American Academy of Pediatrics (AAP) conducted a study on the importance of play in promoting healthy child development. The study's authors noted that today's children were much more stressed, depressed, and busy, and that they weren't experiencing nearly enough time to relax, play, and just be children.[10] This hectic lifestyle can also be spiritually damaging, according to Scottie

May, associate professor of Christian formation and ministry at Wheaton College. She has researched the spiritual development of children and believes that what kids need these days may in fact be the exact opposite of what they are experiencing. "In trying to help our children be the best they can be, we're not so good at creating sacred space for them so they can encounter the presence of the living God," May says. "There is so much constant *doing* right now, so much frantic busyness, instead of sitting in the presence of God, letting the spirit of God speak to them. By doing so much, we're actually neglecting the spiritual formation of our children."[11]

Missional moms strive not to succumb to the extreme cultural pressure to overparent and overschedule their children's lives. They recognize the value of encouraging kids to express their giftedness and talents, not for the purpose of fulfilling an achievement orientation in their lives, but rather as a way to serve God and His purposes. These intentional mothers stand up to the cultural pressures and choose a different course for their children, even if it seems completely at odds with what the rest of the world is doing.

Our family nearly reached a breaking point before we recognized that we were falling into this cultural trap. Two years ago, when our eldest son was in first grade in the local public school, we found ourselves drowning in busyness. On top of school, homework, sports lessons, and music practicing, our son was studying Mandarin on Sundays for two hours after church. Initially, having our kids learn Mandarin seemed like a fun idea, a way to expand their cultural horizons while learning a language that was gaining importance and relevance in our increasingly global society. (I was not the only one who felt this way, apparently; Mandarin-immersion schools have started popping up all over the country, some of them with heavy competition to gain admission.) But as my son slaved away, trying to memorize the utterly unfamiliar characters and wrap his tongue around the difficult tones, complaining all the while, I kept pushing him forward. "This is good for him," I would tell myself. "Someday he will be so glad he did this!"

The Missional Mom

But as the year wore on, I began to realize that my motivation for having my six-year-old learn Chinese was less about furthering his cultural horizons and more about giving him some sort of competitive edge. In the dark recesses of my mind, I hoped that stretching his brain in this way would serve as a kind of mental strength-training program, providing dividends that would last until his first SAT or ACT exam. I'd bought into the cultural trap of pushing kids to achieve—and not for God-glorifying reasons. I'd even rationalized away the conviction to keep the Sabbath holy because there was just no other space in our schedule to fit in the class. When I finally recognized my poor motives, our son was most grateful, as he no longer had to go to Chinese school anymore!

A NATION OF CONSUMERS

Not only are children experiencing stress and pressure from overscheduled and busy lifestyles, but they are absorbing the values of a culture that celebrates excesses, whether it is an abundance of money and possessions or an abundance of choices. It's not enough for Americans to have one option for toothpaste, shampoo, or yogurt—we have to have a plethora of options in an attempt to fulfill everyone's particular preferences. The Oscar-winning movie *The Hurt Locker* features a brief scene that simultaneously amuses and yet offers a biting social commentary about American consumerism. The main character, Sergeant William James, is an Army officer serving with a bomb squad in Iraq. After weeks of hardship in the Middle East, William returns home to his wife and infant son and back to civilian life. He and his family are at the grocery store, and his wife asks him to grab a box of cereal; the next scene shows William standing in front of a typical grocery store cereal aisle, befuddled by the endless rows of options. There is no dialogue or even motion in this scene, yet the stark contrast between his daily life-and-death battles in Iraq versus the near comical nature of this aisle displaying hundreds of boxes is immediately clear. (Businesses do their part to make us believe we need all the options of cereals on the shelves, for example, as they create "product extensions" to help a brand live in perpetuity. What would life be, after all, without Honey Nut/Multigrain/Banana Nut/ Fruity/Chocolate/Apple-Cinnamon/Yogurt Cheerios to accompany the original—and best—plain version?) Not long after this moment, William returns to the battlefield as he has realized that he much prefers the dangers of bomb-squad life over the dangers of mind-numbing American consumerism.

Most of the missional moms I interviewed targeted this relentless consumerism as one of the most insidious cultural pressures they experience. It's extremely difficult to carve a different path for ourselves and for our children when we are so constantly bombarded by consumerism and its inherent pressures. For now, suffice it to say that we must be aware that consumerism is a force to be reckoned with in our lives. Author and speaker Tracey Bianchi writes about the pull of consumerism in her excellent book *Green Mama: The Guilt-Free Guide to Helping You and Your Kids Save the Planet:*

> Our families experience an onslaught of advertising each day because . . . marketers must convince us that we need this stuff. The exact number of ads we are exposed to daily is widely debated (estimates range anywhere from 200 to 3,000 per day). But from buses to bathroom stalls, it seems that every available space our eyes might rest upon has been captured for advertising. Our children learn a myth at an early age: it is best to consume.[12]

Bianchi goes on to explain that these consumeristic urges have been with the human race ever since Adam and Eve spied the one thing they could not have and gave in to its temptation. The challenge for the missional mom is to recognize the things we are tempted to have and our children are tempted to own and to say, "What we have is enough." When missional moms claim with absolute certainty that God satisfies more than any man-made object of desire ever could, their message runs absolutely counter to the marketing ploys of nearly every American company. The missional mom stands against the cultural forces that tell us that "being a good American is being a good shopper."[13]

THE IMPERFECTIONS OF
CHRISTIAN CULTURAL VALUES

To say that Jennifer Jao is a woman of many gifts would be a blatant understatement. Not only is she fluent in five languages, Jennifer is a board-certified physician in pediatrics and internal medicine. She also has a heart for serving those with HIV/AIDS in Africa, which eventually led her to the field of infectious diseases, in which she recently completed a fellowship at the Mt. Sinai Hospital in New York City. Her dreams of eradicating these diseases as well as to bringing humane treatment to those who suffer from them do not stem from personal ambition, but from her commitment to God and to His heart for the poor, the powerless, the shunned, and the sick.

Jennifer is also a mother; she and her husband, Greg, have two young girls under the age of three. When her daughter Madeleine was an infant, Jennifer's responsibilities to her fellowship required that she take a three-week trip to Africa. With Greg's unwavering support for her professional gifts and calling and with the help of her extended family, she was able to make the trip. But as Greg confessed to me while she was away, gently bobbing a sleepy-eyed Madeleine on his shoulder, "Jennifer cried for four straight days before she left, about how she was such a bad mother to be abandoning her daughter like this, no matter how much I tried to tell her that she was no such thing." (In chapter 9, you'll find out more about what happened on Jennifer's trip and how God used her powerfully in the lives of the Africans she met.)

What was the source of the angst Jennifer felt in her heart, soul, and mind as she wrestled with the guilt of being apart from her daughter? To be sure, some of the emotion came from her God-given desire to be with her daughter, whom she loves and whom God has designed to be nurtured and cared for by her parents. But an equal amount of angst came from the tension Christian mothers feel to balance the callings God has placed before them against the message from Christian culture that being good mothers means their lives must only and always be about their children.

Absolutely Christian mothers—and fathers—are called to "train a child in the way he should go" (Proverbs 22:6), and we are given a responsibility to care for these precious gifts God has placed in our lives. But Christian culture has not been immune to the trend of helicopter parenting. Christian mothers find it even more difficult to resist the cultural pull of overparenting when it has been wrapped up in a spiritual package in order to justify it. How can a mother discern which calling trumps another? Ultimately, she has to go to God's Word, where the biblical position is *not* that mothers are to love their families first. On the contrary, Jesus clearly teaches that He takes primacy, even over family.

Mary Ellen Ashcroft, college chaplain and professor of English at Kalamazoo College, writes that "women have been encouraged to idolize their family lives. We are so used to thinking that this is acceptable, even laudable, that we forget that Jesus stood out against this kind of idolatry . . . Jesus points out to His own mother that her calling to be a disciple takes primacy over her job as mother."[14]

Missional moms find ways to affirm their roles as mothers and wives without losing sight of their ultimate calling—to pursue God first and foremost and to live out the mission He has given. There may be stretches or seasons in which the needs of our children take an inordinate amount of our time and energy, especially when they are young, and we need to give space and grace to mothers in those exhausting early years of parenting. At the same time, we must continue to encourage all mothers, regardless of life stage, to continually ask the Lord for his guidance in prioritizing their lives. As long as we are willing to follow His gentle nudges to serve Him in whatever opportunity He presents, we can avoid the trap of idolizing our family to an extent that is not biblical.

"Our greatest and most constant temptation as parents is to unseat the Sovereign from His throne and replace Him with our family," says author Leslie Fields. "We may reason that as long as we do not replace God with ourselves, as long as the God substitutes are God-given—our children and spouse—and we are *serving* and *loving* them, as God commands, then this must be good and acceptable. But God's love is frighteningly exclusive."[15]

AMERICAN AND CHRISTIAN
ARE NOT ONE AND THE SAME

I recently attended a Fourth of July celebration at a large Chicago-area church. The celebration featured a rousing rendition of the theme songs of all the branches of the armed forces, honored current and past military veterans, and encouraged the audience to participate in patriotic standbys such as "The Battle Hymn of the Republic" and "God Bless America." But as much as I enjoyed all the pomp and circumstance, another part of me felt unsettled by the subtext of the celebration: that being a Christian and being an American were one and the same. This is, of course, not the case.[16] But often we get fooled into thinking that being good consumers and competitors, which is ideal for America, is the right way to live.

Wheaton's Scottie May says, "Our churches and our homes are so immersed in the culture of the current lifestyles, which includes materialism, autonomy, individualism, and competition. The biblical context is foreign. For many of us, we're living in the world's culture and we see the biblical culture through the world's culture. We've gotten our lenses turned around. When I can't see any difference between the Christian family's lifestyle and a non-Christian's family, but the same stress-filled pace, we're missing something."[17]

The missional mom recognizes the cultural influences around her and stands against those contrasting with God's plan and purpose for her life. She strives to develop sensitivity to discern which cultural forces run counter to biblical values. And she pursues a life in line with God's ideals, even if it does not look ideal to the world.

Missional moms have discovered what happens when they pursue lifestyles that demonstrate unabashed commitment to their one and only God: their lives reflect the vision Paul describes in Philippians, that Christians are to be "children of God without fault in a crooked and depraved generation, in which you shine like stars in the universe" (Philippians 2:15). In the next chapter, we'll delve more closely into the countercultural values and choices that make the lives of missional moms shine and stand apart from the rest of the world.

CHAPTER THREE

The Missional Mom
Is a Culture Rebel

We have not shown the world another way of doing life.
Christians pretty much live like everybody else.
They just sprinkle a little Jesus in along the way.

SHANE CLAIBORNE

If you have the good fortune one day to be driving west on Massachusetts' picturesque Route 2, right before you reach the state line you will drive into the heart of a college nestled in the valley of the Berkshire Mountains. And if you decide to stay awhile and walk the campus grounds, heading north, you will find yourself navigating a gently sloped hill, shaded by towering trees, straight into a large concrete dormitory named "Mission Park." Most students at Williams College have no idea why the dorm is named as it is, and I myself did not know the history of the name until a couple of years into my time at the school, although every time I headed toward Mission Park I did notice the interesting marble structure located in the grove of trees.

It turns out that the gray marble sculpture, a pedestal with a three-foot globe on top, was a monument to commemorate the "Haystack Prayer Meeting" in 1806, during which five Williams students were caught in a thunderstorm and took refuge in a haystack.[1] The passionate discussion and prayer they had together while in the haystack ultimately gave birth to the American foreign missions movement, as four of the five students dedicated themselves to lives of Christian service domestically and abroad. "Mission Park" is thus named to remember and honor those who took seriously God's call to make disciples of all nations.

As the years went by, Williams and many other colleges in the Northeast lost their original mission to train students for a life of Christian service. The cultural pull away from Christian influence was too great to overcome, which is why my main remem-brance of Mission Park as a student was that it was basically a large party dorm, filled every weekend with undergraduates looking to have a good time. Except for the handful of Christian students who regularly host prayer meetings at the monument site, Mission Park's history and importance has largely been forgotten.

Now that we've recognized and acknowledged that cultural forces can have an enormously powerful sway in our lives, we come to the sobering reality that many Christians remain unaware of these forceful influences or unwilling to stand against these influences. Just as Williams College and other early American colleges founded for the purpose of furthering God's kingdom lost their way, unable to maintain

　　　　　　　　　　　　　　　The Missional Mom

their Christian focus, Christians in large part have lost their ability to discern how modern American culture is shaping them, as evidenced by the lack of discernible difference in the lifestyles of Christians as compared with non-Christians. Missional moms, however, are standing firm against the cultural tides, intentionally pursuing lifestyles that run counter to society's culture—and even counter to the culture of many of their Christian peers. Missional moms have become "culture rebels," refusing to blindly accept the direction today's cultural forces are trying to steer them.

SALT AND LIGHT? OR SOMETHING ELSE?

"If you've been calling yourself a Christian, you should stop."

This thought-provoking sentence appears in the book *The Big Idea*, coauthored by Dave Ferguson, Jon Ferguson, and Eric Bramlett. (Dave and Jon Ferguson are cofounders of Community Christian Church, an innovative, multisite church in Naperville, Illinois. Dave is the husband of Sue Ferguson, who was introduced in the last chapter.) Let me share a few more choice nuggets from this book:

The last thing the mission of Jesus Christ needs is more Christians.

Eighty-five percent of the people in the United States call themselves Christians. But how are those 85 percent doing when it comes to accomplishing Jesus' mission? Research tells us that North American Christians . . .

- Are no more likely to give assistance to a homeless person on the street than non-Christians.
- Are no more likely than non-Christians to correct the mistake when a cashier gives them too much change.
- Will choose elective abortion as often as a non-Christian.
- Divorce at the same rate as those who consider themselves non-Christians.

In fact, when the Barna Research Group did a survey involving 152 separate items comparing the general population with those who called themselves Christians, they found virtually no difference between the two groups . . . If the contemporary concept of a Christian is of someone who is no different from the rest of the world, is Christian really the word you want to use to describe your willingness to sacrifice everything you have to see God's dream fulfilled? No way.[2]

The Ferguson brothers are not trying to be heretical, but they are calling attention to the fact that Christians are often hard to identify in today's society—or if they do stand out, they stand out for less-than-admirable reasons. For example, novelist Anne Rice recently announced on her Facebook page that she had decided to "quit being a Christian" because she no longer wanted to belong to a "quarrelsome, hostile, disputatious, and deservedly infamous group." Neither invisibility or infamy reflects what Jesus would want to see from His Bride, I imagine.

In contrast to many of today's Christians, Jesus was both alluring and yet as rebellious against the prevailing culture as He could be. He challenged just about every cultural norm of His time, by fraternizing with those who were thought to be "unclean," refusing to bow to pressures of legalism from the ruling religious leaders, and championing and supporting women and children throughout His ministry. And yet, unlike the way Christians are perceived today, Jesus drew such a following not just because He performed amazing miracles but because He lived in a manner utterly unlike anything people had ever seen. His words are as radical and challenging today as when He first uttered them. Take, for example, the famous Sermon on the Mount in Matthew 5. Here are the words and phrases describing those who will be called "blessed" in Jesus' value system:

- poor in spirit
- mourning
- meek
- hungering and thirsting for righteousness
- merciful
- pure in heart
- peacemaking
- persecuted

This is not the kind of list that resembles the American dream, which proclaims the right of every American to have "life, liberty, and the pursuit of happiness." Author, activist, and speaker Shane Claiborne writes about this supposed ideal: "I know plenty of people, both rich and poor, who are suffocating from the weight of the American dream, who find themselves heavily burdened by the lifeless toil and consumption we put upon ourselves."[3]

And yet for those who follow the countercultural way Jesus prescribed, the benefits are compelling. These Christ followers:

- receive the kingdom of heaven (mentioned twice)
- experience comfort
- inherit the earth
- will be filled with righteousness
- receive mercy
- will see God
- are called sons of God

These blessings sound completely opposite to the burden and oppression, as Claiborne describes them, felt by those laboring after the American Dream. Yet how many Christians today wake up and pray that God will help them become poor in spirit or persecuted? How many feel thankful when conflicts arise so they can be peacemakers or grateful for a loss so they can mourn? How many of us really want to be the kind of people with the qualities

Jesus lists in the Beatitudes? It's hard to ask for things such as greater persecution or mourning in our lives. When we grasp how difficult it is to live as Jesus asks, we can better understand why today's Christians do not look much different from the rest of the world. Somehow we have gotten our concept of what the true Christian life is all about confused with the cultural messages of our day. As Os Guinness writes in his book *The Call*, "For many believers the Christian life is now the good life."[4] And, sadly, he does not mean that in a positive way. Jesus puts it even more forcefully, describing what the fate should be of those Christians who no longer exhibit the qualities of "salt and light" described in Matthew 5: "But if the salt loses its saltiness, how can it be made salty again? It is no longer good for anything, except to be thrown out and trampled by men" (Matthew 5:13).

One reason we may have lost the desire to pursue the kind of Christianity the Bible calls for is that we have not understood the concept of sacrifice. By today's cultural standards, "sacrifice" should be avoided, except if you are a member of the armed forces or anyone else who serves in potentially life-threatening situations, in which case we applaud your willingness to sacrifice for the rest of us. But *all* Christians are called to a life of sacrifice. When Jesus told the disciples to follow Him, He did not give them the option to select what parts of the Christian walk to accept or avoid. We cannot embrace all the loving, comforting verses of Scripture without simultaneously owning the difficult ones such as, "If anyone would come after me, he must deny himself and take up his cross and follow me" (Matthew 16:24, Mark 8:34, Luke 9:23).

Related to the idea of sacrifice is the idea of discomfort. Making sacrifices and denying oneself usually means experiencing discomfort of some kind. But it's hardly human nature to seek out the uncomfortable option! We naturally want to live in neighborhoods and homes that are comfortable, go to churches that feel comfortable, and build relationships with people who make us feel comfortable. In Dave Goetz's book *Death by Suburb*, an unabashed critique on Christian living in suburbia, he tells the story of a woman who "yanked her first child out of school after his kindergarten year, transferring him to a Christian grammar school. The woman apparently felt uncomfortable with all the kids from 'the apartments' in little Johnny's class. 'Too diverse,' she said. 'Besides, don't kids at the Christian school end up getting better SAT scores?'"[5] This woman was unable to see that her decisions were driven less by a Christ-centered perspective to love others and seek first after His kingdom and more by cultural messages to seek after success and comfort.

I confess that seeking after comfort is certainly an issue for me. When I was a child, my parents would often take time on spring Sunday afternoons to drive around nice neighborhoods in our suburban Maryland town and visit houses that were for sale and open for viewing. They dreamed about a day when they could afford such houses, which was their concrete way to establish that, as immigrants, they had successfully achieved the American Dream. I remember one fabulous residence with a beautiful, calming, rectangular fountain in the foyer (fish not included with house), reminiscent of the Reflecting Pool at the Washington Monument. The living room featured a spectacular wall of windows overlooking a wooded, private backyard sanctuary. The house had more bedrooms and bathrooms than our family of four would ever need and a basement wine cellar stocked with hundreds of vintage bottles (wine not included either). The price tag for this piece of serenity and luxury? $1.2 million, and that was back in the 1980s!

Even at a young age, I could appreciate that $1.2 million was a lot of money. Although I never thought of myself as an overly materialistic person and even told my parents that "I don't need to live in a house like that," I would also repeat a mantra I have carried with me since then: "I just need to make enough to be comfortable." Now I am coming to realize that my desire for comfort reflects a spiritual fragility, an under-willingness to live a life of sacrifice and potential discomfort to which Jesus is calling me. Once you begin to desire to be comfortable, your measuring stick of what is "comfortable enough" starts getting bigger and bigger. It's much harder to reverse your upwardly mobile direction and pursue a less comfortable option. The more comfortable we become, the more comfortable we want to be.

The great irony is that as we seek after a life comfortable by the world's standards, we become more and more weighed down by the burden of seeking it. Dave Goetz tells another story of a man who complained about a speaker he had heard at church. The speaker had challenged the men to "get out of their comfort zones," to which Dave's friend said, "What comfort zone? I work all day in the corporate world, try to be a father and husband, and tithe and give some time to the church. If there's a comfort zone in that, I want to know about it!"[6] But sometimes the reason today's Christians take little comfort from their everyday lives is that they are pursuing the wrong kind of comfort. Some people feel the great weight of trying to "keep up with the Joneses," and work more and more hours to provide what they think their family must have in order to be comfortable.

Jesus, as you might imagine, has something to say about where true rest and comfort come from. Consider His words about His yoke in Matthew 11:28–30: "Come to me, all you who are weary and burdened, and I will give you rest. Take my yoke upon you and learn from me, for I am gentle and humble in heart, and you will find rest for your souls. For my yoke is easy and my burden is light." Shane Claiborne says about this passage, "People take that to mean that if we come to Jesus, everything will be easy . . . [but] if our lives are easy, we must be doing something wrong."[7] According to the passage, we attain Jesus' promise of encompassing spiritual rest once we put on Jesus' yoke—and yokes, if you have ever seen them on oxen, for example, don't seem very comfortable to wear. As we follow Jesus' way of life, He will most certainly challenge us. Taking on Jesus' yoke is *not* comfortable. Life will be tiring, it will be costly, and it will be hard. But, in another paradox of the Christian life, what may initially seem difficult and uncomfortable will result in "rest for our souls." We will gain the incomparable spiritual peace that Jesus promises, whatever our particular circumstances might be.

Missional moms understand that living sacrificially and eschewing comfort as a goal will result in their lives looking difficult and challenging to those of us unused to such a countercultural approach. As you will see in the next section, real-life missional moms have made some tough choices, but even as they live with certain discomforts they experience the goodness of life in a way that sustains them more than any dream house ever could.

THE PARADOX OF SACRIFICIAL LIVING

On a lovely warm day last spring, I had the opportunity to spend time in Southern California with a triumvirate of amazing missional moms, three women whose lives reflect this idea of embracing Jesus' yoke instead of pursuing what the world sees as comfortable. And yet what amazed me is that what appear to be sacrifices to me are, to them, just a normal part of their everyday lives. Each of these women had experiences to share about how they demonstrated sacrificial love and kindness toward others. They all had experienced the sense of heavenly affirmation and rest that only comes from taking Jesus' yoke upon them, as opposed to seeking after worldly comforts.

I met first with Rachel VerWys in the town of Bellflower, about twenty miles southeast of Los Angeles. Bellflower started to show signs of urban decay in the 1990s as residents left for more attractive housing options in surrounding locales, such as Orange County. Rachel is the mother of three children five years old and younger, and she and her husband, Ryan, are heavily invested in the community. Ryan runs the local nonprofit Kingdom Causes, which seeks to bring transformation to Bellflower as "God's people live out the Great Commission locally."

Rachel and her family have done everything from picking up random strangers who need a place to stay to taking care of a homeless family who wandered into the Bellflower park one day. Rachel brought the mother and children to her minivan and gave them everything she could—clothes, food, flip-flops, and even her four-year-old son's favorite Bob the Builder toy. "These kids had no toys, or anything, and I knew it would be hard for my son, but he had so many more at home," Rachel says. "Six months later, we saw them and my son remembered that they were the family we had helped. Those moments stick with our kids."

Soon Rachel and Ryan will welcome the family of a church member into their home; the husband is from the Philippines and just became a citizen; his wife and son are scheduled to join him in the U.S. soon. "For us, it's very natural now to open our home to others. If I have an extra room, I think that of course we should invite people in. It's all God's in the end for us to give," Rachel says. She and her husband believe strongly in having a hospitable home, and they deeply desire for their children to understand that they have been blessed in order to be a blessing to others.

On my next stop, I met our mutual friend Katy White, who attended Williams College along with me. Katy, I have learned, has become quite the missional mom in the twenty years since I last saw her, when we were both premedical students slaving away in science courses. She has since become the doctor she had always planned on becoming. I hadn't known, in our college years, that even then God had begun to shape her heart for those who are poor.

After going to India and Mexico during and after college, Katy's heart was profoundly moved by the poverty she encountered. She knew from that point on she would want somehow to be involved in ministering to impoverished communities. Today Katy and her husband, Bill, live in the town of Paramount, just west of Rachel's town of Bellflower. They have two kids, an eleven-year-old son and a nine-year-old daughter. Katy works part-time as a physician in an inner-city Christian clinic; her dream is to launch a health clinic in neighboring Compton.

One of the most missional ventures Katy's family has undertaken was "to have a troubled twenty-year-old young woman live with us for a year. It was tough at times, and she did not end up making good choices in her life, unfortunately—she's now in jail. Was it a risk? Yes. But we grew a lot as a family and were blessed in the process." Like Rachel, Katy feels strongly that her kids should learn at a young age how important it is to serve and love those who are the most in need. "The kids know it's so much a part of my heart that they always tell people, 'Our mom always wants to be with those who are poor.' I talk about it a lot. I want them to have that passion too."

The last of the three women I met is Tonya Herman, who lives in Compton, the town just west of Paramount, where Katy lives. Because of gang violence and criminal activity, Compton has earned a negative reputation; in 2008, it was named one of the top twenty most dangerous cities in the U.S. But Tonya has lived in and served the community for more than ten years, together with her husband and two kids, who are eleven and nine years old. On the day of our interview, Tonya was getting ready to celebrate the college graduation of her unofficial godson Ramiro, one of two brothers she took into her home once college became a reality for Ramiro. The boys had previously lived in a small apartment with other family members, and Tonya's family offered another option. "We wanted to provide an easy environment while they were in college, a room all their own where they could have a quiet place to study and do schoolwork. We also wanted to be totally available to help them through the college process in whatever way they needed," says Tonya. "There was no better way to do that than having them in our home."

Despite the costs of this long-term hospitality, Tonya has absolutely no regrets. She appreciates what living in Compton and learning to share resources has done for her and for her family.

"The white middle-class community is so much about 'my space' and 'my stuff,' but that's not the way it is in this community. Nobody had his own room growing up in this community. It is good to challenge some of those cultural values people have, that everyone should get his own room," Tonya says. Not only will her godsons get college degrees, but her own kids will grow up valuing the Hermans' lifestyle of sacrificial hospitality. "My kids know that is what we are called to do. I've always prayed they would think it was a privilege to live in our community. And they do," Tonya says.

RISK BOLDLY

It is easy to be humbled by the lives of women like Rachel, Katy, and Tonya. The sacrifices each made and the discomfort each must have experienced in demonstrating such hospitality can be mind-boggling. At one time our family considered helping another family by providing housing to a friend struggling with mental health issues. On the one hand, we wanted to be gracious and loving and we had a room to spare for the purpose. But my husband and I also wrestled with the risks involved, especially for our children. We wanted to better understand the ramifications of making the offer before we made it, and we dragged our feet in making a decision. By the time we had finally agreed to open our home, the need was no longer there. I felt that our doubt and indecision had prevented our family from accepting the opportunity to serve and love others.

In any step of faith and sacrifice, you run the risk that the result will not turn out as you might have hoped. Katy experienced disappointing results with her twenty-year-old female boarder, who made poor choices and ultimately had to leave the Whites' home. Anytime you put yourself on the line for others, you risk being hurt in some way, shape, or form. But I have learned from listening to the stories of missional moms that the risk does not just signify the potential for hardship. Risks also signify the opportunity to stretch one's faith and lean on God's provision in ways you could not have imagined. As these missional moms took on risks and sacrifices, an amazing thing happened: their risks and sacrifices stopped feeling risky and sacrificial and became everyday life.

"There are simply no guarantees what pursuing a calling will cost," writes Joy Jordan-Lake in her book *Working Families: Navigating the Demands and Delights of Marriage, Parenting, and Career.* "But then, what would be the point of adventure? And faith?"[8]

Have today's Christians lost the joy of taking risks in life? In our desire to live comfortable lives, do we insulate ourselves and our kids against any possibility of harm, so much so that we see faith-stretching as an exercise to be avoided more than to be welcomed?

A recent example from my own experience has helped me start to understand how faith-stretching risks are part of living missionally. I attend a church that recently moved to a city with a lower-income, under-resourced population. As part of the mercy and justice team of our church, I helped plan a community health fair to reach out to local residents. My main responsibility was to promote and publicize the event, so another team member and I planned to distribute flyers door-to-door in neighborhoods considered "hot spots" in the community.

One Sunday morning, Michelle and I headed for the apartment complexes down the street from our church, a seemingly endless stretch of single-story, four-unit structures I had previously only known as the "Division Street apartments." My impression of these buildings was not particularly favorable, and I admit that a part of me was fearful. But the sun was shining, the work was calling, and we armed ourselves with colorful neon flyers and started our visits.

The longer I was in the complex, making contact with curious residents (especially children) who poked their heads out to see what we were doing, detouring around the bicycles and other paraphernalia that signaled the presence of kids, and saying hello to senior citizens sitting on their front stoops or working judiciously on the tiny grassy portions of land allotted to them, the more my fearfulness was replaced with a desire to interact with the people who lived in these cramped, dilapidated apartments. I noticed that, in many cases, what must have been at most a one- or two-bedroom apartment had as many as eight names written on the mailbox. I smelled the odor of breakfasts being prepared and heard the sounds of televisions in the background, interspersed with the chatter of families beginning their day. Division Street no longer represented an unknown, fear-inducing location; instead, Division Street became people. I left the complex with my mind filled with pictures of the faces of the people I had met and feeling grateful that I'd had the chance to visit the apartments and get a sense of who lived there.

When the day of the community health fair arrived, a number of people from Division Street attended our fair because of the flyers Michelle and I had brought to the apartments. I felt like the little boy who watched Jesus multiply his small offering of five loaves of bread and two fish into a great feast. Despite my needlessly big fears, I took a small step of faith, and God honored that risk. Next year I will take my kids with me, so that something that once felt risky for me won't feel the slightest bit scary for them. We will all grow in embracing a missional lifestyle together.

As we begin to take these small steps of faith, showing God we are open to risks and sacrifices for Him, God begins to stretch us more and more to have even greater impact on the world. For someone like me, who is just beginning to understand what it means to be missional, the example of the countercultural lives of Rachel, Katy, and Tonya can feel daunting; I wonder how I could ever be anything like these women! It may take me some time to be able to let complete strangers stay in my house and reduce my preference for privacy and space. But I'm also intrigued by the testimony of the grace and blessings these women seem to experience. On the day I met her, Tonya offered a reminder to me of the great paradox in Scripture about what happens when you give your life away:

> People might say "you're so noble," but I am selfish and struggle with materialism like so many Americans do. But I have received abundantly more in the last twenty years than I have given out. I don't want to live my life any other way. I have found my life in pouring it out. From the outside looking in, it might look like there's a great cost, but I don't feel that's been the case. It's been well worth the cost. I don't mean to sound super-spiritual, but it's really true: you give your life away and you receive it back.

As we'll see in the following chapter, opening our eyes to the realities of the world is a great tool to help us break out of our comfort zones and "rebel" against the cultural forces that pull us away from God's mission for our lives.

CHAPTER FOUR

The Missional Mom
Engages in the
Needs of the World

*"In the end there are only two attitudes
which Christians can adopt toward the world.
One is escape and the other is engagement."*

JOHN STOTT

If you live in a house built in the 1960s or later, most likely you live in a house without a front porch. With the exception of newer homes constructed with front porches to restore a past architectural relic, most modern homes sport backyard decks instead of front-of-the-house porches. The disappearance of the front porch coincided with an increasing privatization of American family life. As cars began to pollute streets with noise, as air conditioning became a common fixture inside, and as televisions drew people away from their yards, households found fewer and fewer reasons to stay outdoors and chat with neighbors.[1] It was easier just to escape into your own personal haven and not deal with the rest of the world. The appearance of backyard decks only contributed to the self-containing trend; you could enjoy the outdoors in the privacy of your own yard (especially if your yard was fence-enclosed) and never have to interact with a soul.

In 1996 the Walt Disney Company (WDC) acted in contrast to this trend. The first residents of Celebration, Florida, moved into their pristine new town, developed by WDC as a new experiment in urban planning. Celebration was a community meant to evoke the nostalgia of the early twentieth century, when towns were small and people walked everywhere, socializing on one another's front porches. Nearly every home in Celebration was adorned with that retro architectural structure. The city planners hoped this new community would promote neighborly interaction and bring families out from their privatized retreats. As it turned out, people hardly spent any time on those porches, fearing the encephalitis-bearing mosquitoes thriving in the surrounding swampland.[2] Not even the spirit of Mickey Mouse could inspire residents to battle the pests when it was easier to escape into air-conditioned, bite-free comfort.

ENGAGE OR ESCAPE?

We all need opportunities to escape the pests of life, whether they are disease-bearing mosquitoes or issues of larger consequence. Jesus Himself retreated from the world to experience the renewal that only being in the presence of God could bring. However, Jesus made it clear that God's intention is not for us to remain sequestered, but to take God's transformational power to the world.

Our comfort-craving culture, however, makes it very challenging to choose engaging with the world over retreating from it.

The Missional Mom

When my mail carrier delivers a Pottery Barn catalog depicting impeccably designed rooms as well as a report from Voice of the Martyrs describing the ongoing persecution that so many warriors of the faith battle every day, it takes Herculean effort for me to opt for the disturbing stories in the VOM magazine and throw away the catalog. (Not to mention, it is nearly impossible to get off those catalog mailing lists!) But, as John Stott says so wisely and succinctly, Christians face a choice either to turn their backs on the world or to engage in the world's needs. And when a Christian chooses to close his or her eyes to those needs, it is no small tragedy.

One way missional moms live counterculturally is to resist focusing only on what is happening within the walls of her own house and instead to take notice of the needs outside her doorstep. Certainly missional moms give their families high priority, and certainly there are seasons of life, particularly when children are young, when it's difficult for a mother to do much else *but* focus on her family. Mothers are called to "watch . . . over the affairs of her household" (Proverbs 31:27) and to be a nurturing, supportive presence for family members. But managing one's household is not the same as retreating from God's mission for Christ-followers to care for the world. God has strong words for His people when they spend too much effort building their own households at the expense of His house.

Author Carolyn Custis James insightfully analyzed the word "helper" or "helpmeet" as it has been translated from the Genesis 2:18 passage ("The Lord God said, 'It is not good for the man to be alone. I will make a helper suitable for him.'") What I learned from her book *Lost Women of the Bible* is that the Hebrew word for helper is *ezer*, which she describes as a "powerful Hebrew military word" that implies being a "warrior." She writes, "We are all *ezers*—chosen by God to soldier alongside our brothers . . . advancing Christ's kingdom in the hearts of people all around us."[3] In other words, Christian moms are not people who passively escape from the world, but instead they engage in it, battling alongside the men in their lives to bring God's kingdom from the not-yet to the here-and-now. *Ezer* is a proactive, strong word, reflecting God's hope for women to take initiative to bring about change. In contrast, when His people do not act in this manner, God takes them to task, as He does in the book of Haggai.

WHEN THE PEOPLE OF GOD
ESCAPE, NOT ENGAGE

Haggai is an Old Testament book you can easily miss if you are flipping the pages of your Bible too fast. Haggai is a short book, one of the minor prophets near the end of the Old Testament. But if you take a look at this book, you will find it incredibly instructive for us today. In particular, the book of Haggai demonstrates God's great displeasure when His people ignore the needs He wants them to address and focus instead on building their own households.

To understand Haggai, we must go back to the time of Solomon's reign. Along with the wisdom for which he was well known, Solomon's legacy was the construction of God's temple, a magnificent structure that, unfortunately, did not endure as the Israelites turned away from God and ended up exiled in Babylon while their glorious temple lay in ruins. Nearly fifty years after the destruction of the temple, God moved in the heart of King Cyrus of Persia to send the Israelites back, and they began to rebuild the temple. But then the Israelites stopped, succumbing to outside pressure from neighboring countries who feared what would happen if Israel successfully restored God's temple. So instead of engaging in the continued mission to build the temple, the Israelites abandoned the project for sixteen years, with only the temple's foundation completed. The next king of Persia, Darius the Great, was also willing to let the Israelites continue their work, so the fact that God's people were not progressing with His temple was entirely their own fault. This is when the prophet Haggai comes into the story.

Through Haggai, God's message to the Israelites is clear: "Is it a time for you yourselves to be living in paneled houses, while this house remains a ruin?" (Haggai 1:4). The phrase "paneled houses" implies luxury or royalty, so not only have the Israelites been ignoring God's house, they have been putting a great deal of effort into building their own domiciles. Later, God implores once again:

> Give careful thought to your ways. Go up into the mountains and bring down timber and build the house, so that I may take pleasure in it and be honored. You expected much, but see, it turned out to be little. What you brought home, I blew away. Why? Because of my house, which remains a ruin, while each of you is busy with his own house.

During the sixteen years after they abandoned work on the temple, the Israelites demonstrated that God's mission was not as important to them as focusing on their own lives. They were fearful of their surrounding enemies and culture, but instead of engaging in a battle against those pressures, they chose to escape into their paneled houses and ignore the clear calling God had given them to rebuild His temple. The consequence for this abandonment of their calling, in addition to earning God's displeasure, is that their labors produced very little fruit.

Finally, God's words through Haggai broke through. The Israelites did eventually heed God's warnings and turned their attention to rebuilding the temple, which they were able to finish in four years once they stayed on task.

What does this passage have to do with our lives today? For me, the questions that Haggai raises for us are:

1. Are we putting the priorities of our lives in the right order?

2. Are we allocating our resources in a God-honoring way, with regard to the way we tithe, use our time, and treat our material possessions?
3. What are ways God wants for us to build His household today?

The first two are good questions for moms (and dads!) to be asking themselves continually. We can easily slip away from God's intent for how we live, so we must be vigilant in evaluating how we use the resources He has given us, as we acknowledge that *all* that we have is from His hand.

Part of the effect of our consumer-driven culture is that Americans feel they cannot be satisfied until they have either more possessions or more wealth to gain those possessions. Even the richest in our exceedingly wealthy nation feel they could use more. In his book *Rediscovering Values*, Jim Wallis discusses a study by wealth-management firm PNC Advisors, which discovered that "rich people almost never feel secure in their wealth . . . Those with a net worth of $500,000 to $1 million said they needed $2.4 million. Those with a net worth of $1 million to $1.49 million said $3 million. And those with a net worth of $10 million or more said $18 million." As Wallis keenly observes, "If our security and our happiness rest in our net worth, enough really never is enough."[4]

At the same time, America is experiencing an extended period of economically challenging times, and many families are sincerely struggling to make ends meet. But even this time of budget-stretching and belt-tightening can have a positive effect on how we think about what we have and what we spend. When you feel discouraged about the assets you have, visit the website www.globalrichlist.com. My friend Al Hsu brought the site to my attention when he posted a blog entry a few years ago.[5] You can enter in your household's total income and discover where in relation to the rest of the world you are in terms of wealth. For example, if your household earns $30,000 a year, you are in the *top 8 percent* of the richest people in the world. Plugging in my own numbers was an eye-opening and challenging exercise for me. It brought to mind the words of Jesus in the gospel of Luke: "From everyone who has been given much, much will be demanded" (Luke 12:48).

In addition to regularly assessing how our family is using its resources, we've found it helpful to review how tightly or loosely we are holding on to our material possessions. We occasionally ask our children, "If God asked you to give Him your _____ (fill in the blank with a favorite or special toy), what would you answer?" The intent here is not to portray God in a negative light but to gently help our kids wrestle with the question. We're glad they get to keep those much-loved toys, but we want the boys to learn that they cannot put even their most favorite possession above their love for God. (Adults could benefit from asking themselves this same question as well!)

To answer the question about how God may want us to build His household in contemporary times, I'd like to turn to another passage, Isaiah 58. In case you are thinking that building God's household means getting involved in typical Christian religious activities—say, fasting—God has some strong words here as well to share with us:

> Yet on the day of your fasting, you do as you please
> And exploit all your workers.
> Your fasting ends in quarreling and strife,
> And in striking each other with wicked fists.
> You cannot fast as you do today
> And expect your voice to be heard on high.
> Is this the kind of fast I have chosen,
> Only a day for a man to humble himself?
>
> (Isaiah 58:3–5)

Of course, fasting can be an important personal spiritual discipline. But rather than offering up true expressions of worship, God's people were going through the motions of a fasting day, giving lip service to one day of worship but reflecting no true dedication to God's ways in the rest of their behaviors. God saw right through their false religious expressions and then laid down the challenge, through Isaiah:

> Is this not the kind of fasting I have chosen:
> To loose the chains of injustice
> And untie the cords of the yoke,
> To set the oppressed free
> And break every yoke?
> Is it not to share your food with the hungry
> And to provide the poor wanderer with shelter—
> When you see the naked, to clothe him,
> And not to turn away from your own flesh and blood?
>
> (Isaiah 58:6-7)

God implores His people to look after the needs of others, to address those issues rather than getting caught up in discord among themselves or in unjust behavior or in meaningless religious activity. God tells His people to open their eyes and see what is happening around them, then to take action and make a difference. His commands are just as relevant today. The missional mom embraces this call on her time and attention instead of shying away from it. She acts as God's warrior of light and love to those who most desperately need it.

HOW GOD OPENED THE EYES
OF TWO WARRIOR MOMS

I know two missional moms whose stories demonstrate their willingness to confront the realities and needs they see instead of walking away. Both were moms living typical suburban lives, but once their eyes were opened, they found ways to engage rather than retreat! These women provide two examples of the wide and varied ways God can transform "soccer moms" to have an impact in the world.

Kirsten Strand used to live in Naperville, that city described as one of the "best small cities to live in the U.S." She chose her church, Community Christian Church (CCC), for its strongly outward-oriented mentality and desire to have impact on the surrounding community. At first, Kirsten decided to volunteer at CCC by helping to develop a ministry reaching out to those in need. "I'm a clinical psychologist by training," Kirsten says. "I had no ministry training, I had no community development training, but I wanted to do *something*." Kirsten had an open heart and mind to see what God had in store for her, particularly in the context of serving those who were in poverty. And then He opened her eyes.

Kirsten had to drive to the neighboring town of East Aurora for a meeting in a local restaurant. As she made her way westward from Naperville, she was astonished to see how quickly the landscape and environment changed. "I literally felt I had crossed a railroad track. You could see such a visible difference between the two towns. I was appalled that there was such a difference just ten miles down the road," Kirsten remembers.

She could not shake the memory of what she had seen in East Aurora and went home to research and learn what she could about the community. "The more I learned, the more upset I was that we as a church could have ignored this. I was disgusted with myself that a community so close in proximity to me had children who were living a completely different reality than that of my kids. It became a passion for me, trying to rectify the injustice of it all, when our God is a God of justice. We had a responsibility to do something about it." Little could she imagine where God would ultimately lead her and her family as she began to respond to the call to serve those who were impoverished and underserved in East Aurora.

As Kirsten's children grew and she continued to work on building a compassion and justice ministry within CCC, Kirsten had an experience that further opened her eyes to what God intended for her and her family. "I will never forget the day my oldest was in second grade. He came home and said, 'I can't go back to school unless I have a pair of Heelys.' Heelys are those sneakers with wheels in them, and at the time they cost $80 a pair. I thought, 'If this is happening in Naperville in second grade, what will happen when they get older?' With all the materialism and the competition in Naperville, there are evils here every bit as much as there are in East Aurora."

Kirsten and her husband, Scott, had come to a crossroads. They sensed God was calling them toward a greater commitment to the community of East Aurora. The question became whether or not they had the willingness to follow God's leading. Kirsten says, "We decided that if God was calling us to this, He knew we had children, and He would take care of them. We had to be willing to lay down that cross and say, even if the absolute worst happens, that we would be able to accept it."

It took two years of planning, praying, and thinking through the decision, but in 2007, Kirsten and her family, including her nine-year-old and seven-year-old sons, moved to East Aurora. Kirsten had progressed from seeing the needs in the world that God wanted her to see to actively participating with God to do something about those needs, ultimately resulting in her family's relocation. "I felt I could no longer preach reaching out to the community of East Aurora if I didn't live it myself," Kirsten says.

Today God is using Kirsten and her family to make a tangible difference in the lives of others in East Aurora. Kirsten is the full-time director of the ministry God led her to start at CCC, called Community 4:12, which both serves under-resourced communities in suburban Chicago (such as East Aurora) and also helps to

The Missional Mom

alleviate extreme poverty around the world. Kirsten did not turn away from the needs she saw but opened her heart, soul, and mind to accept the calling God gave her and continues to take concrete steps of faith and action to address those needs.

By moving out of Naperville into East Aurora, Kirsten feels that her whole family has benefitted from the change, especially her kids. "In Naperville, it was so hard for my kids to find others to play with—everyone was always so overscheduled or inside with their video games. But here, kids are outside all the time, or you can call one five minutes beforehand and ask 'Do you want to do something together?' and they'll be right over," Kirsten says. She also discovered that leaving behind a well-resourced community for an under-resourced one has been a blessing for her as well: "There is such a more relaxed atmosphere here. It's allowed me to be better mom, better wife, better person. I don't obsess or stress about the same things I used to before. I just felt so at home immediately when we moved here."

Around the same time that Kirsten was working on the launch of Community 4:12, a man was touring the heartland of America with a caravan of performers, medical experts, and celebrities. The man's name was Bono, of U2 fame, and he was bringing his Heart of America tour to Wheaton College in Illinois, one of the stops in his effort to raise awareness and mobilize people to do something about the HIV/AIDS epidemic in Africa. Edman Chapel, the site of the rally, has a capacity of two thousand people, but it was standing-room-only as the crowd gave a thunderous ovation to welcome Bono and company.

One of the people who managed to get into Edman Chapel was actually not a student, but Bono fan-*cum*-suburban mom Shayne Moore. An alumna of the college and a Wheaton resident, she put her two young kids to bed, then sat in the darkened auditorium and confronted a reality she had never known much about before. "I considered myself an educated woman, but I did not know those statistics about AIDS and HIV. Why didn't I know?

Why weren't we talking about this in our churches? I was angry when I left that presentation," Shayne says. "And Bono didn't mince words. He said, 'If the church isn't going to respond, who will respond?' I took those words to heart."

For Shayne, anger led to action. Her eyes had been opened to the realities of the AIDS pandemic, and she was not turning back. She connected herself with a local AIDS network and learned about the policy side of AIDS awareness, prevention, and treatment. Then Shayne became one of the original members of the ONE Campaign to Make Poverty History (www.one.org), which grew out of the Heart of America tour and which now has more than two million members. Her passion for fighting issues of global poverty were noticed by the leaders of the ONE Campaign, who recruited Shayne to be their "non-celebrity spokesperson." In 2005 and 2006, the ONE Campaign sent Shayne to the G8 Summits in Scotland and Russia to continue her public role as a spokesperson to urge world leaders to care about global poverty. What had started as an eye-opening personal revelation had transformed over time into opportunities for activism on a global scale.

The pivotal moment for Shayne occurred when she saw evidence that her activism had actually resulted in change. She was in Kenya on a short-term missions trip in 2005, working in a rural hospital and learning firsthand about AIDS diagnosis and treatment in Africa. While she was there, a woman came to pick up her AIDS medication, antiretroviral drugs that have been effective in combating the effects of the deadly disease. Shayne was curious to know where the drugs had come from and asked the clinic nurse. "The Kenyan Government got the money from PEPFAR," she replied. (PEPFAR stands for the U.S. President's Emergency Plan For AIDS Relief.)

In that moment, Shayne had an epiphany. She had lobbied for PEPFAR through her work with the ONE Campaign, asking President George W. Bush to sign it into law.

I had picked up the phone and called the White House about this—they actually answer the phone when you call!—and now here I was in Africa, seeing a woman leaving with her life-saving medication due to the passage of a law that I helped advocate for. Organizations pay big dollars to have lobbyists rally for their cause, but I realized that for that woman in Africa, I was her high-powered lobbyist. The Scripture that came into my mind was, "Be a voice for the voiceless." Me, a suburban, Christian mom—I'm the best she has. I stumbled into making a difference on a global level, but anybody can do this. Anybody can make a phone call.

One of the challenges Shayne experienced in her transformation from typical suburban mom to *ezer* as she engaged in the fight to eradicate global poverty is that she received pushback from friends and even family members who did not understand why it was important for her to be involved in these activities. "The message I was hearing at times was that to be the good Christian wife and mother you can't have anything going on outside of the home. The thing that brings you the most respect in the evangelical subculture is your title as a mom," Shayne says. "But I knew God was calling me to do these missional things, like going to Africa or lobbying at the G8 summits. I didn't have any models from my faith tradition saying you can be both/and, but I want my daughter to see a mom who would follow God first, wherever He called, a mother who could both love her kids and battle global poverty. I've learned there are many different ways you can be both."

Shayne has recently written a book about her experiences as an ordinary suburban mom taking on the issues of global poverty called *Global Soccer Mom* (Zondervan). Hers is a wonderful story of how, if you are open to seeing the needs of the world around you and willing to take concrete steps to make a difference, you actually can make that difference. The subtitle of Shayne's book is *Changing the World Is Easier Than You Think.* I highly recommend it. When Christians take a stand and move from apathy and passivity to action, the world notices. If you look at the June 2007 issue of *Vanity Fair* Magazine, you will see a full-page photo of a group of key ONE Campaign supporters, including Matt Damon, Ashley Judd, Rick Warren, Speaker Nancy Pelosi, Senator Bill Frist—and Shayne Moore.[6]

BUT I'M NO WARRIOR!

At this point, you may be saying to yourself, "I can't. I can't! How can I be like Kirsten and Shayne?" But the point is not for you to be like Kirsten or Shayne! Not all moms are called to pick up their families and move to a needier neighborhood; not all moms are meant to lobby in front of world leaders. These are simply stories about women who said, "I am willing. And *God* can." They are stories about women who did not retreat but kept their hearts open to see the needs God showed them.

The temptation is to say, "Being a 'warrior mom' is just for those specially selected women with super-extraordinary strengths." But when God created the *ezer* for Adam, it was not a one-time creation or one limited to a handful of women. All women were created with God's intention for them to be *ezers* in our world. How those warrior women will battle for God is going to manifest itself differently from mom to mom, but they will all share the common quality of willingness to do what God asks.

There is no formula for how to become a mom who engages with the world. But here are four steps to consider if you would like to move from a posture of retreating from the world into one that addresses its needs.

1. Place yourself where you can see, hear, and become aware of the needs around you. Read newspapers and magazines to keep current with what is happening in the world. Sign up to be a part of the ONE Campaign (www.one.org). The organization does a great job informing the public of major legislation that needs support and educating members about global issues related to poverty.

The Missional Mom

Read *Half the Sky* by Pulitzer Prize-winning writers Nicholas Kristof and Sheryl WuDunn and *The Hole in Our Gospel* by World Vision president Richard Stearns, named the 2010 Christian Book of the Year by the Evangelical Christian Publishers Association. I highly, highly recommend both books for compelling information on global needs (although I warn you that the content is not always easy to stomach, particularly in *Half the Sky*).

2. **Pray** that the Holy Spirit would speak to you if there is a particular issue He wants you to address or confront. Ask specifically that the Spirit would move in your heart in a strong way so you can discern God's leading. Missional church authors Alan and Debra Hirsch write in their book *Untamed*, "Jonathan Edwards says that if the heart is left unmoved by God, no spiritually significant action can, or will, take place."[7] Prayer is the key to opening our hearts to be moved by God so that we can ultimately make a difference for His kingdom.

3. **Probe** to gain a deeper understanding of a particular issue that is calling for your attention. Both Shayne and Kirsten responded to the tugging they felt in their hearts by doing more research to understand the issue better. This will help you to discern whether the tugging is in fact a calling to a need that God may want for you to address. If it is, the continued exploration will fuel and further your desire to take action.

4. **Participate** with God in helping combat the issue with concrete steps of action. These actions can be as small as picking up the telephone or signing an online petition in support of legislation; they could be bigger steps of faith as you grow in your knowledge and understanding of how God wants to use you. As you begin to take concrete steps of faith, your way will become clearer regarding how God will use you to make a difference in the world.

One of the challenges of telling stories of people in hindsight is that we can become daunted by the eventual outcomes without realizing that what drove the story forward were small acts of obedience. But when Shayne in an act of faithfulness made that phone call to the White House, she wasn't doing something any woman couldn't do. She had the wonderful experience of seeing a tangible result when she was halfway around the earth in Kenya. But even if we don't get the opportunity to see the fruits of our labors, we can trust God for the results. Missional moms have taught me that we are responsible for everyday faithfulness, and when we act in faith God turns our ordinary offerings of obedience into the extraordinary. As you sense the Spirit of God asking you in that quiet, still, voice, "*What can* you *do*?" the key is not to ignore that voice but to step out in faith, doing what you can, knowing God will multiply those efforts as only He can.

I had one of those "What can you do?" experiences recently, when I was surfing the Web one evening. Somehow I stumbled onto an article about children in Bangladesh who were eking out a miserable living, pounding on batteries to extract the reusable core inside.[8] The work incessantly exposed the children to black dust that was horrible for their lungs and bodies, but for many of these children it was the only way they and their families could survive.

What can you *do, Helen*?

I thought about the gifts I have to offer. I enjoy both writing and working with PowerPoint. So I created a presentation designed specifically for children, to teach them about the needs in the world and give them ideas for how they can help. The presentation is called *God Cares for Bangladesh*. You can download it for free from *The Missional Mom* website at www.themissionalmom. com/resources. You are welcome to distribute it and share it with anyone you wish. If you feel so moved, you can use the links online to sponsor a Bangladeshi child or donate to organizations that devote resources to Bangladeshi children. This feels like a paltry offering given the needs, but it is a beginning. Although I may not see exactly how God will use funds that go toward this cause, I know that He can take even the smallest offerings of faith and multiply them. Meanwhile, I look forward to finding out one day, on the other side of heaven, how God used my small offering.

I encourage you to keep your eyes, ears, hearts, and minds open to where and how God might want to use you. You may never relocate your family to a poor neighborhood or fly off to Africa, but God can use you in big and small ways, if you will let Him. One way to start is by trying to be attuned to the many needs right around you. As you will discover in the following chapter, moms can be especially well-suited for loving their neighbors.

CHAPTER FIVE

The Missional Mom Doesn't "Do Evangelism"

Preach the gospel always. When necessary, use words.
Attributed to ST. FRANCIS OF ASSISI[1]

Something is wrong when a person claims to belong to Christ and yet fails to love others.
ED STETZER and PHILIP NATION

The title of this chapter may initially seem heretical, but bear with me. Grab a pencil and piece of paper, and take a few minutes to write down whatever comes to mind when you hear the word *evangelism*. There's no need for full sentences, just jot down the most immediate words that pop into your head.

Now open your Bible, one with a concordance; it doesn't

matter what version. If you prefer to use a computer, you might try an online Bible site such as BibleGateway.com. Search for the word *evangelism*. Then write down what you find the Bible says about it next to your earlier thoughts on the word.

Are you surprised by what you discovered?

It may be hard to believe, but the word "evangelism" does not appear in the Bible. You can find the Greek words *euangelion*, meaning "good news," or *euongelistes*, meaning "evangelist," numerous times in Scripture. However, *evangelism* is a word that has emerged over time to describe the processes and programs of how today's Christians share the good news of Jesus Christ. In contrast, the early church never seemed to concern itself with how to "do evangelism." For these Christians, evangelism was a natural part of life, not an obligation or a task relegated only to those who considered themselves evangelists. The early church knew that their good news had to be shared, even if it meant death. For them, evangelism was so woven into the fabric of being Christ-followers, so integrally a part of their lifestyle, that no word was necessary to describe it.[2]

Nor, do I imagine, were these early Christians armed with a list of things to say or do, or a specific prayer they were supposed to pray to ensure that someone had crossed over the invisible line and become one of the spiritual family. Why? Because this was not the way Jesus Himself modeled sharing the Good News.

It's a valuable exercise to explore the misconceptions that have developed over the years about evangelism. In contrast, Jesus' example informs new ways of thinking about evangelism. Today's missional moms are demonstrating what it means to evangelize without "doing evangelism."

When you made your list of words that came to mind when you thought of evangelism, words such as "scary" or "hard" may have appeared on your list. Perhaps, then, you will find it freeing to let go of the idea that you must "do evangelism." After all, why

The Missional Mom

would any of us want to do something that is, clearly, not in the Bible?

WHY CONVERSION IS NOT ENOUGH

Tongue-in-cheek aside, although *evangelism* as a word doesn't appear in the Bible, examples abound in Scripture of evangelistic activity. We are all certainly called to share the Good News of Jesus Christ. But for many of us, particularly those of us from the evangelical tradition, "doing evangelism" has come to mean following some sort of program or process with a definite end goal (conversion), a task that for many of us seems unnatural and forced. A number of years ago, when I was serving as a college parachurch ministry worker, I participated in an evangelism training session. One of the training exercises encouraged us to summarize the Christian message in five minutes, then in two minutes, then in fifteen seconds. (We discovered the trick to accomplishing the last task was to just recite John 3:16 very fast.) But how effective a strategy would that really be for helping to bring someone to a life-changing knowledge of the Lord? If I walked up to a random stranger and spouted John 3:16 at him, he would probably brush me aside dismissively. My "victims" would categorize me together with the banner-wielding believers they regularly see in sports stadiums displaying the same verse: "There go those Christians again. If that's what they want to believe, it's fine for them, but it's not for me." Evangelism done outside the context of a relationship rarely carries much weight.

Some believers have certainly come to faith in Christ through the ministry of a large gathering such as a Billy Graham crusade, in which one key evangelist preaches the message, building up to a pivotal moment—the call to make a decision for Christ. In fact, *Decision* is the name of the official magazine of the Billy Graham Evangelistic Association, reflecting the importance given to that moment when someone actively chooses to follow Jesus. Millions of people around the world have become Christians through crusade ministry, and my intent is not to downplay the important role these gatherings have played in the lives of so many. But the limitation of the crusade model of evangelism is that it focuses so much attention on the "decision" and not enough attention on what happens to the new believer *after* the decision. It's almost as if we are selling Christianity-as-Eternal-Life-Insurance rather than as the entry point to a lifelong journey with Jesus.

According to the data that says potentially as many as 25–40 percent of adults who used to be Christians have fallen away,[3] conversion has not been enough to sustain commitment. Evangelism has to be about more than just getting people to sign a card or raise their hands. I find the words of Jesus in Matthew 7 particularly challenging, as it calls into question the evangelical tendency just to get people over the decision line in order to assure their salvation. Jesus makes it perfectly clear that salvation is reflected not in a moment but in one's lifestyle. As He plainly says, "Small is the gate and narrow the road that leads to life, and only a few find it . . . Not everyone who says to me, 'Lord, Lord,' will enter the kingdom of heaven, but only he who does the will of my Father who is in heaven" (Matthew 7:14, 21). Jesus makes a clear distinction between those who say they believe—and those who live like they do.

We live in a time when Christians do not act in ways that are particularly distinctive from non-Christians. Is there something about the evangelistic process by which many people have become Christians that makes a difference in their long-term spiritual journey? Let's look at how Jesus handled "evangelism" for some clues.

When Jesus called His first disciples, He never relied on a single moment of decision. Rather, His directions were clear: "Come, follow me . . . and I will make you fishers of men." He did not seek a conversion moment and then walk away. Instead, Jesus invited them into an *ongoing* relationship with Him, one that gave them

The Missional Mom

opportunities to walk alongside Him and see how He lived from moment to moment, through weeks and months, and ultimately years. This call on the follower's whole life, with a wise mentor to lead the new follower, is certainly a different conversion model than the moment-of-decision model. Can you imagine how different those statistics about falling away from the faith would look if every person who made a decision for Christ were paired with another person, a mature Christian who would walk alongside him or her in life and help the new believer reach maturity?

NEW WAYS TO THINK ABOUT EVANGELISM

The idea that evangelism is less about getting people to convert and more about walking alongside people so that they can witness Christianity in you is not only a much more accurate depiction of what evangelism truly is, but also one that aligns well with who we are as women and mothers. Relationships are a significant part of our lives, whether we are relating to our family, our friends, or other people God brings into our path. Whenever we are bearing the light and love of Christ and demonstrating that Jesus matters in how we are living, we are being evangelists. It's not the same as "doing evangelism." It's living in a manner worthy of the gospel, in view of others who can see that being a Christian makes a difference in us, and there is no more powerful witness in the world. Adopting this vision for whole-life evangelism does not mean we never take the time or risk to present the gospel message to someone else, even a stranger; proclaiming the gospel is absolutely a critical part of bringing people to a saving knowledge of Jesus Christ. But proclamation works best when it is done hand-in-hand with demonstration. That is to say, the words I speak about God's good news mean more to someone who can see that my words are true because of the way I live, the way I behave. Letting people see God's truth at work in my life means letting them into my life. Evangelism happens in the context of relationships.

Living evangelistically in this way, however, requires that you might have to let go of some of your former ideas about "doing" evangelism and replace them with a fresh vision for what it means to bring people to Christ. Here are some ways this approach is different.

It takes time. Helping people to see Jesus in you is not a one-time event, but a long-term process that can take well more than weeks or months. It can take years. It can take *decades.* Ken Fong is the senior pastor of Evergreen Baptist Church Los Angeles, a multiethnic, missional church community in Pasadena. In his book *Pursuing the Pearl,* he writes, "When we state that our goal is to enable more unconvinced people to become Christians, what we have in mind is far more expansive than leading them in the Sinner's Prayer and leaving it at that. Instead, we hope to initiate them into the lifelong pursuit of the pearl of great price. . . . Too many programs or approaches do not afford the unconvinced much dignity, because they do not allow them enough room to let a relationship with Christ emerge gradually and naturally."[4] In other words, if you are in relationships with non-believers, give them time to come to a point of embracing Christ without pushing for a decision before they are truly ready.

It may be a process, not a moment. We live in a postmodern world, in which making choices to follow Christ rarely happens based solely on rational and cognitive acceptance. Although people will always become Christians through genuine repentance and conversion, for many this will be a longer process and they may not clearly identify the time of their new birth. You may find believers today who cannot pinpoint a precise "moment" when they came to faith in Christ. Instead, as they are influenced by their relationships with Christ-followers, they are made a new creation in Christ. They begin to change and adopt the same beliefs and values, without being able to identify a moment of conversion. In his book *Evangelism Outside the Box,* Rick Richardson writes that "belonging comes before believing. . . . Most people do not 'decide'

The Missional Mom

to believe. In community, they 'discover' that they believe."[5] In today's culture, helping people embrace Christianity is less about convincing them and more about inviting them into your community and helping them to see and find Christ in you.

It's about the center. Missiologist Paul Hiebert, a former professor at the Trinity Evangelical Divinity School, has influenced many missional thinkers with a different way of representing what it means to be a Christian. He called it the difference between being a bounded-set thinker and a centered-set thinker. A bounded-set thinker imagines a boundary separating non-Christians and Christians, with Christians "in" the circle and non-Christians "out" of it. With this model in mind, the goal is to get the non-Christians over the boundary and into the circle with the rest of the Christians (see the left side of the figure below).

However, in centered-set thinking, the most important question is not "Are you in, or are you out?" The most important question becomes, "Is your life heading toward or away from Jesus?" So in centered-set thinking, the focus is on the trajectory of a person's life, with the understanding that, as Richardson says, many people today may not even realize they are becoming more Christlike. But the more they discover about Jesus, the more they see Him reflected in the lives of His followers, the more they want to become like Him as well. With this model in mind, our role as Christians is to help those we come in contact with to move along

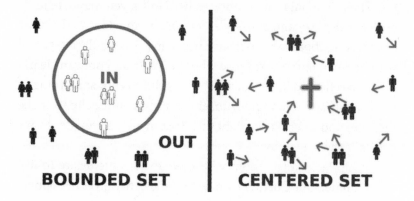

BOUNDED SET | **CENTERED SET**

that trajectory toward Jesus, no matter what their exact faith status might be.[6]

It's not actually about evangelism. Let's revisit the core of what it means to be missional. Being missional is about the Great Commandment and the Great Commission. Jesus' words are beyond clear as he sends out his disciples in preparation for his own departure from earth. "Therefore go and make disciples of all nations," he says in Matthew 28. Go and make *disciples.* Not "go and make converts"! The essence of what it means to help people adopt the Christian faith is not to "do evangelism" to them. The mission is to *disciple* them. Missional church leaders Alan Hirsch and Debra Hirsch write about the difference between conversion and discipleship in their book *Untamed: Reactivating a Missional Form of Discipleship*:

> If each believer understood discipleship in this way and then took their biblical mandate seriously, we would have lots of people growing and becoming more and more like Jesus—and hopefully at some point coming under his lordship. It's not our role to convert them, but to disciple them. Conversion is God's business. How much better would the world be? And the fun thing is that in many cases those who haven't yet accepted Jesus as Lord may have no idea that they are being discipled! [7]

The missional mom embraces her God-given mandate to be both a *disciple of* and a *discipler for* Christ. She doesn't shy away from talking about Jesus, but she does so in a way wholly integrated with her own life so that those who do not know Him can clearly see Him reflected in her lifestyle. Evangelism is not something to do; evangelism is living purposefully and intentionally to make disciples and to bring the light of Christ in all that you do. Evangelism is the way to live!

Stacy Paolella is a mom whose life exudes the desire to live every moment for Christ. Her holistic perspective gives her opportunities to influence others around the clock and demonstrates that "doing evangelism" isn't an occasional separate activity, but a lifestyle. For part of the year, she is on Young Life staff reaching out to teen moms, but she does not see her ministry life as the only place where she touches people's lives with the love of Christ.

> My "mission field" is my daily life, the grocery store, the post office, the play groups. It is every situation and place I find myself in every day. It means loving my family as a missionary, sharing Christ with them in word and deed. It means intentionally becoming friends with people who do not know Jesus so that I will have the opportunity to love them and live a real faith before them. It means making decisions about money, time, and resources that will glorify Jesus every day. We view every relationship, every situation, every event in our lives as a chance to "live" the gospel of Christ.

Stacy's children have learned to follow her example, as they pray for their sports teammates or invite friends who are not Christians to church-related activities. "Every Thursday when my older son attends his youth group, we are picking up a carload of kids he has very purposefully invited," Stacy says. "He intentionally invites kids who do not go to any church." As Stacy has learned from watching her children embrace the call to disciple their friends, it's never too early for a child to become not only a disciple of but a discipler for Christ.

It will pull you out of your comfort zone. Some of you may find this redefinition of evangelism freeing and more natural. Still, the shift to infusing every part of your life with the goal of sharing Christ may be intimidating and uncomfortable. That is okay! It often feels unnatural and uncomfortable when we push ourselves to be proactive enough with other people to share in each other's lives. With a cultural norm of increasingly privatized lives (remember the porch vs. deck analogy?), people are so busy and stressed that they have a hard time making or welcoming opportunities for interactions with others. Reaching out despite our tendency to "cocoon" has become much harder.

Rae Ann Fitch is a mother and part of a missional church community called Life on the Vine in Long Grove, Illinois. For Rae Ann, motherhood became the catalyst for missional action after she had her son, Max, at age forty. At first, she found that being a mom was an isolating, challenging experience: "I had been living my own life, concerned primarily about my own needs, and then a baby came into our lives and changed everything!" she says. To combat her feelings of loneliness and isolationism, she took action to push herself into an unfamiliar situation and joined an e-mail list of other mothers in her community, most of whom are not Christians. As a result she has had many opportunities to build relationships with women who she would not have met otherwise.

"I don't consider myself an extrovert. It's hard to go out and introduce yourself and try to strike up relationships with other moms. Everybody is in her own little world. A lot of people don't want to be known, especially out here in the suburbs," Rae Ann says. "But now I have opportunities to try to be the love of Christ for someone in need. I'll listen, I'll strike up conversations about real life and try to go deeper than talking just about potty training. It can get uncomfortable at times, being with so many people with different worldviews, but the experience has opened opportunities to speak into people's lives, and I know I'm called to be authentic with people and shine the love of Christ."

Rae Ann's experience raises a wonderful point about the advantage all mothers have as they seek to be missional: motherhood itself provides many connecting points that can build bridges to other women. If you are willing to push out of your comfort zone just a little bit, you can find so many opportunities right around your neighborhood into which you can bring a Christian presence.

Now that we've considered the ways traditional definitions of evangelism and missional ideas of evangelism differ, a good question might be, "What do I do next?" In his book *The Monkey and the Fish*, named one of *Leadership Journal*'s ten best books of 2009, pastor Dave Gibbons of Newsong Church (based in Irvine, California, but with sites all around the world) shares three questions that have guided him in ministry and decision making, and they seem particularly relevant in helping us think about the topic of bringing the love of Christ to the world: 1) What is my pain? 2) What is in my hand? and 3) Where is Nazareth?

What is my pain? Gibbons writes, "I'm discovering that most people can't relate to our achievements or successes. However, most people can relate to our pain and our losses, our disappointments and suffering."[8] Patsy Chavarria, a forty-seven-year-old mother of three kids who lives in Lakewood, California, has experienced the truth of this statement. Motherhood was the catalyst God used to bring change into Patsy's life, as she began examining her lifestyle and realizing she did not want her kids to grow up in an environment that could be harmful for them. "Socially, I used to drink a lot. I had a potty mouth. My husband and I used to indulge in recreational drugs, but that's all completely out now! I did not want my kids to be around those kinds of influences," Patsy says.

A little more than ten years ago, Patsy turned her life over to Christ, after being a part of the Alpha Course[9] at Emmanuel Reformed Church (ERC) in Paramount, California. She loved the Alpha experience so much that she continued to be involved, leading courses for others struggling to understand the Christian faith. Patsy feels a key reason that God has given her a heart for this ministry is that she can speak to others from a position of understanding pain.

"God hobbles us for a reason, to draw ourselves closer to Him; we come in broken, not even realizing that we *are* broken," Patsy says. "When we're broken and vulnerable before one another, it allows others to share their hearts and be comfortable." She and her husband have shared with the Alpha group members about serious struggles in their marriage and how the consequences of certain decisions from their days before knowing Christ have continued to affect them. Patsy has seen how God has used those challenges to help others understand the struggles they are going through. "My husband and I are able to give others hope as they see our story. We are able to show that you can be angry at each other but then you can forgive."

For Patsy, "doing evangelism" has nothing to do with traditional evangelistic goals. "I have asked so many people to come to church, but nobody comes. That's not evangelism to me. I think evangelism is really about sharing your life and loving other people. As they know they are loved, they become reeled in to Christ. I'm always asking people if I can pray for them—such as my pizza delivery lady or the tow truck driver who came to my house or the woman at the checkout counter—God brings people to my path, and Christ comes out." Patsy exudes the amazing, natural aura of deep connection to Christ, and her natural desire to care and pray for people is alluring. At the end of our conversation, she asked to pray over me as we prepared to part ways, and I could easily see why she has become the "chief Alpha evangelist" for ERC. It's not because she "does evangelism," but because she so clearly loves other people and lets them into her life and her past areas of brokenness and pain.

What is in my hand? Gibbons explains that much of the time, we focus on what we don't have instead of what we do have, especially when God has a job for us to do. Moses makes a good example. His initial response to God's call was by no means an enthusiastic, "Yes, Lord!" Gibbons encourages us to ask ourselves, "What are the gifts you have to offer others?" Patsy's gifts are her ability to share her points of pain, her prayerful spirit, and her love for introducing people to Jesus. Everyone has her own particular set of strengths, experiences, hardships, relationships, and contexts God has uniquely designed for His purposes. A key to understanding how God wants to use you is to ascertain what makes you uniquely you.

Susan Arico has given a great deal of thought to her unique calling, given her gifts and experiences. She is both a stay-at-home mom as well as a part-time consultant and contributor to GiftedforLeadership.com, a blog for Christian women leaders. With her experiences in business, she brings the no-nonsense perspective of someone who can be rational and objective when necessary, but at the same time she is personable, extroverted, and relational. "I can look at things differently from other people in my stage of life," Susan says. "My friends ask me to help them understand what is happening in their marriages, or in their parenting, or in their priorities. Our relationships are built on trust, so I am able to say things in a way that people will hear them."

Susan has parlayed these strengths into developing relationships particularly with mothers who rely on her for advice and counsel. "If you see others struggling in an area where you've gained some wisdom or perspective, it's good to turn around and help," she explains. "The relationships can come from anywhere, from playgroups, from the mom's group at church, or even from e-mailing friends from different parts of the country." The combination of her role as a mother as well as her unique gifts have enabled Susan to become a discipler of other mothers, and her gifts and skills have helped her to bring people closer to Jesus, which is the whole goal of discipleship.

What are your interests, gifts, and skills? Perhaps you have a gift for craftwork and you love scrapbooking. Maybe you have a gift in music, or photography, or sports; perhaps you are a counselor or an excellent cook. Maybe you have a gift in teaching, in business, or in organizational leadership. Perhaps you are incredibly wise and discerning. Whatever your gifts and interests, think of them all as tools for the Lord's use, for the purpose of connecting you with others and giving you the opportunity to help them grow closer to Jesus.

Where is Nazareth? At this point, our focus shifts from the people immediately around us to a potentially broader circle of influence. At the very beginning of the book of Acts, Jesus issues His final directive to His followers, that they be His witnesses "in Jerusalem, and in all Judea and Samaria, and to the ends of the earth." He gives them the big vision of the scope of his ministry, which indicates Jesus' desire for all people of the earth to have the opportunity to learn about Him and respond.

Sometimes, though, it is easy for us to ignore ministering to those groups of people who need it the most. Gibbons reminds us of the statement in the gospel of John that Nathanael makes about Jesus: "Nazareth! Can anything good come from there?" (John 1:46). Nazareth wasn't much like the desirable community of Naperville, where I live. Nazareth was more like Kirsten Strand's neighborhood of East Aurora, a place people didn't want to be, the place with the bad reputation. Gibbons asks, "Where is the other side of the tracks in your city or region? In other words, who are the marginalized or the outsiders near you, people whom you feel pain for? Who in your community is the outsider, the misjudged, the misunderstood?"[10] As you willingly and faithfully open yourself to God's leading about marginalized places and people, you could find yourself on an amazing journey. Such a journey happened in the life of Carisa Hinson and her family.

Carisa was a typical suburban mom, living in Charlotte, North Carolina. She and her husband, Frank, had gone with their church on a mission trip to Jamaica, and they loved the experience so much they made time to be involved regularly in missions work at their church. But there was one "Nazareth" Carisa could not face; she was terrified of going to an inner city and was absolutely certain she would never be called to ministry in an urban setting. "Something about inner city culture, maybe it was the fear of everything the inner city represents—drug dealers, prostitutes,

The Missional Mom

racism, welfare—scared me to death. I just couldn't imagine ever going there."

Little did she know God had other plans. A church missions trip to Mexico had to be scrapped at the last minute due to problems with the mission agency, and the team decided instead to participate in the work of an inner-city ministry in Philadelphia. "I cried for two hours after that meeting," Carisa says. "I was just devastated, and I almost did not go. My fears were nearly irrational, but finally in the end, I decided to go."

What completely took Carisa by surprise is how she felt from the first moment her team's van drove into the Kensington neighborhood in Philadelphia, Pennsylvania. The team had arrived much later than expected and accidentally ended up on an abandoned street, surrounded by vacant lots and trash everywhere, prompting fear on the part of many team members—except for Carisa. "I cannot explain it, but for some reason, the moment we drove down that street, I no longer had any fear. We arrived on a Saturday; by Wednesday I had the intense sense of calling that God wanted us here."

As a confirmation to Carisa's sense of calling, her husband, Frank, had been experiencing exactly the same thing. Within six months of their return to Charlotte, Carisa, Frank, and their two young children moved into the inner city of Philadelphia as a missionary family to seek the transformation of the lives God placed in their path. God had brought the Hinson family to the Nazareth where Carisa had never wanted to go. What was truly amazing was how quickly her perspective changed.

"I laugh because all those people I feared before—the drug dealers, the prostitutes—we know many of them now. We have prisoners and heroin addicts in our home all the time because my husband leads the recovery ministry here. These are people we count as friends, who we have Thanksgiving with, who my kids will hug and call 'Uncle.' These are people I love," Carisa says.

Carisa also says, "The word 'evangelism' scares me to death.

The thought of going to my neighbor and handing over a tract still scares me. But I've learned that evangelism is not about holding a piece of paper and having 'the talk.' It's about living our lives in the presence of others so that they can see Christ in us." What is fascinating to realize that as Carisa and her husband have embraced a "Nazareth" Carisa never thought she could, her children have eagerly accepted their neighborhood, not as a Nazareth of their own, but as their home. The more mothers stretch themselves to be missional, the more their children thrive in a missional lifestyle as the norm and not the unusual.

Many of us will never have an experience as dramatic as Carisa's. But we all need to be asking God a question we may never have asked Him before: *Where is the Nazareth where You want me to serve?* The missional moms you will meet in the next chapter have taken this question very much to heart, loving and serving "the least of these."

CHAPTER SIX

The Missional Mom Loves "The Least of These"

Let my heart be broken with
the things that break the heart of God.
BOB PIERCE, founder of WORLD VISION

The story of a "missional mom" won an Oscar. The movie *The Blind Side* featured Sandra Bullock in her Academy Award-winning role as Leigh Anne Tuohy, a Memphis mom and interior decorator who takes in a homeless teenager she sees walking the streets one evening. The film is based on the true story of Michael Oher, whom the real-life Tuohy family welcomed into their home and eventually adopted into their family.[1] Oher went on to college and was then drafted by the Baltimore Ravens to begin a career in professional football.

What moved me most while watching the movie was seeing how Leigh Anne's heart begins to break for Michael as she gets to know more about him and his past. In one such scene, after Michael has been sleeping on a couch at the Tuohy house for a while, Leigh Anne decides it is time to give him his own bedroom, so she brings him upstairs and shows him around. He moves with uncertainty in the room, too scared to touch anything, and Leigh Anne attributes his tentative behavior to his never having had his own space. "Never had one before," Michael says, looking around. Leigh Anne thinks this is confirmation of her suspicions and asks, "A room to yourself?"

Michael shakes his head. "A bed."

Leigh Anne's face, turned away from Michael but visible to the viewer, registers shock, an understandable response from a wealthy, suburban, Christian mom, as well as for most movie viewers. Few of us can fully grasp the plight and pain of those who represent "the least of these" in our world. The movie is full of such small but meaningful moments that demonstrate how Leigh Anne's heart is affected, as Michael becomes for her and her family not just the recipient of a charitable act but a deeply loved member of the family. Through the example of Leigh Anne's life as depicted in this movie, and in the real-life story Leigh Anne and husband, Sean, share in their book *In a Heartbeat: How Cheerful Giving Changed Our Lives*, we learn a valuable lesson: there is a big difference between serving the poor and loving the poor. God calls us to do the latter.

As missional moms build on a model of evangelism based on relationships, their focus naturally turns to the second of the two Great Commandments: What does it mean to love our neighbors as ourselves? Who are our neighbors, and what does loving them entail? If we take a closer look at what the Bible says about these questions, we may find more than we were expecting.

The Missional Mom

A DIFFERENT WAY TO THINK
ABOUT LOVING OUR NEIGHBORS

"Who is my neighbor?" the lawyer asks Jesus in Luke 10, prompting Jesus to respond with the familiar story of the Good Samaritan. What is thought provoking about this parable is not just the negative way religious leaders such as priests and Levites are characterized, but also the protagonist Jesus chooses for His story: A Samaritan plays the central role. In Jesus' time, Samaritans and Jews were two ethnic groups with great hostility toward one another. No one would have faulted the Samaritan in this story if he had chosen to ignore the plight of the beaten Jew in his path. What is the point of Jesus' parable? He is trying to teach His followers that He wants us to take initiative with the very people we might be inclined *not* to love or get involved with. This is the radical nature of who Jesus was, as He demonstrated time and time again in loving those considered the rejects of society—tax collectors, prostitutes, lepers, to name a few—in tangible, compassion-filled ways. Loving those who love you, as Jesus says in Luke 6, is not where the power of the Christian witness lies. But when we love those who are difficult for us to love, that is when the true heart of the gospel comes through.

Who are people that you find most difficult to love? Perhaps like Carisa Hinson in the last chapter, you fear certain inhabitants of the inner city: drug dealers and addicts, prostitutes, and gang members. Some of us may find it hard to empathize with the poor and the homeless. Others may struggle to care for people from a different racial or ethnic group or tribe. Who makes up this category of people for you? Who are the people you can't imagine taking the time to build relationships with? Then ponder this radical notion: Those may be the very people God is calling you to seek out and love.

When you reach completely out of your comfort zone, taking a risk of faith in obedience to His calling, then God's glory is most clearly revealed. In her devotional guide *Sharing God's Heart for the Poor*, Amy Sherman writes about how the typical American congregation has lost the "agitated posture" that comes from being intimately acquainted with poverty and suffering. "Face-to-face ministry among the poor, though, can stimulate within us the growth of an oh-so-needed 'holy discontent.'"[2] As we put ourselves in situations in which "loving our neighbor" is a challenge, we are stretched in ways we could not have imagined. We discover that our mission is less about doing the right things for God and more about becoming the people God intends us to be.

WHY GOD CARED SO MUCH FOR THE POOR, AT-RISK, AND OPPRESSED

Along with following Jesus' command to love our neighbor as expressed in the parable of the Good Samaritan, Christians also have to take seriously God's clear injunctions throughout Scripture for His people to love those who are considered "the least of these" in our world—the poor, the hungry, the oppressed, the naked, the widow, and the orphan, to name examples of those on whom God shows particular favor and concern. Jesus Himself reflected this same care for those on the margins of society in His earthly ministry, and He clearly expressed His expectations that His followers would demonstrate a similar lifestyle. Arloa Sutter, executive director of Breakthrough Urban Ministries and author of *The Invisible: What the Church Can Do to Find and Serve the Least of These*, writes:

> True followers of Christ would be recognized by their efforts to provide food, water, and clothing for the needy and by looking after those sick and in prison. Those who love Jesus would love the ones Jesus loves, the world he came to die for. Christians would be known for their love for the poor, the despised, the social outcasts.[3]

In other words, the authenticity of our faith will be reflected in our lifestyle choices, and not just in areas of personal piety or evangelism, for example. God's judgment as to whether we deserve to hear "well done, good and faithful servant" will also be based on how we treat those who are experiencing the greatest needs in our society. What makes the difference between an initial decision to serve Christ—and *truly* serving Him? As our hearts experience the life-changing work of the Holy Spirit, we become more able and open to understand God's heart. Our connection with Him helps us to care for things He cares about and love the people He loves.

But when we ignore those for whom God expresses so much concern in Scripture, not only do we risk disappointing God and not attaining His full favor on Judgment Day, but we also risk stunting our own spiritual development. Sutter writes, "I have rarely heard of caring for the poor as a scriptural discipline, yet it seems to me, according to passages of Scripture like . . . Matthew 25, where Jesus speaks of caring for the needy as if we were caring for Him, that this is a discipline that needs central focus in our Christian tradition and practice."[4]

Although we irrefutably become a child of God when we first understand that Christ died for our sins, that moment is not an end to our spiritual development, but just the beginning. As we truly grow in our relationship with and knowledge of Jesus, we will naturally find ourselves drawn to serve and love those whom He served and loved. As we immerse ourselves in God's Word and become sanctified into His image, we will begin to define "the good life" the way Jesus defined it: a life poured out for others, particularly for those who need our love the most.

"Proclaiming the whole gospel, then, means much more than evangelism in the hopes that people will hear and respond to the good news of salvation by faith in Christ," writes Richard Stearns, president of World Vision, in his book *The Hole in Our Gospel*. "It also encompasses tangible compassion for the sick and the poor, as well as biblical justice, efforts to right the wrongs that are so prevalent in our world. . . . And if this was Jesus' mission, it is also the mission of all who claim to follow Him. It is my mission, it is your mission, and it is the mission of the Church."[5]

COMPASSION FOR THE LEAST OF THESE

I like Stearns' phrase "tangible compassion." How does the practice of tangible compassion apply to God's mission for mothers? The word "compassion" comes from two Latin roots, *com* meaning "with" and *pati* meaning "suffering." The word essentially means "entering into the suffering of others."[6] "Tangible" compassion speaks to me of physical and emotional presence. It's the kind of compassion that takes you actually into the presence of the person you hope to care for, so he or she experiences your love and care in an immediate way. Jesus demonstrated tangible compassion when He was "filled with compassion," as described in the gospel of Mark, then touched the leper who had been an outcast from society and who probably could not even remember the last time anyone had touched him.

"Tangible compassion" means you are not just giving your money and resources, although financial support is certainly one way to start demonstrating care for the "least of these." God calls us to more than donating from a distance. God is calling us to spend time with those in need, living alongside and suffering with them. Tangible compassion happens when you know the "least of these" by name, in a personal way, not letting the ways you are different from each other become a barrier to your growing relationship. Tangible compassion engages not just your pocketbook and your prayers, but your *heart.*

As many of us know, loving others is much easier said than done. What are the barriers that usually keep us from being able to engage "the least of these" in a compassionate and loving way? We've already considered the challenges Americans' busy lifestyles

The Missional Mom

and desire for comfort can pose to leading missional lives; our tendency toward self-absorption and privatizing our lives can also affect our willingness to reach out to those with the greatest needs. But there are other barriers that emerge when we start thinking about serving those who are poor, underserved, and oppressed. Let's examine some of those obstacles and see what can we learn from missional moms who have begun to overcome these barriers.

We think those who are poor deserve the situation they're in. Perhaps we would never say these words out loud, but even if the sentiment isn't often expressed, it is commonly felt. A bit of personal soul-searching may reveal to you that you might be one of those who believe, for example, that those living in poverty should just try to find a job of some kind and start building a better life for themselves instead of living off welfare checks. Arloa Sutter, the founder and executive director of Breakthrough Urban Ministries in Chicago, admits she used to think this way. "But then I realized that many have been crippled from the start, being born into poverty, being born into families where they weren't cared for or nurtured. It's a downward spiral they get into."

Arloa gained a deeper understanding of the homeless as she began to spend more and more time with them. Through her church, she initially launched the ministry in a storefront, offering food, clothing, showers, and basic employment training. Arloa was struck by the stories of abuse and neglect she heard from those who started coming, stories that gripped her heart and changed her perspective on the sufferings of the poor. While she has been serving through the ministry of Breakthrough, Arloa has raised two daughters in the city, starting when they were three and six years old. Today she lives in East Garfield Park, a struggling community on the west side of Chicago. She understands intimately what happens as you fill your life with opportunities to be among those who are considered "the least of these."

"As you hear their stories, as you get to know them personally, as you hear their struggles and see their brokenness, you begin to understand the issues so much more clearly and realize how many more resources you yourself have been given," Arloa says. She explores the blessings that come from connecting the people and resources of the local church with those in need in her recent book called *The Invisible: What the Church Can Do to Find and Serve the Least of These.*

Michael Oher, the teenager depicted in *The Blind Side* who is homeless when the Tuohys find him, had a mother addicted to crack cocaine and a father who disappeared soon after he was born and whose body is ultimately found when Michael is a teenager. No aspect of Michael's homelessness and poverty could possibly be considered his fault. Without any stable parental influences in his life (before he meets Leigh Ann and her family), without even a place he can consistently call home, it seems impossible to expect he could have a chance at surviving and thriving. Although the Tuohys recount in their book *In a Heartbeat* that Michael Oher had the tenacity to survive and thrive even if he had not been taken in by their family, countless other young people have no place to call home, no consistent education, no possibility of the footing they need to lead a stable life—through no fault of their own.

In contrast, although I grew up in a family that had its own financial struggles due to my parents' status as recent immigrants to the U.S., I was still surrounded by advantages that were easy to take for granted—three square meals a day plus snacks, water anytime I needed it, a roof over my head, clothes to wear, access to all the books I wanted through weekly library visits, and parents who, regardless of their financial status, did all they could to give me the best possible education. I cannot take credit for having these advantages any more than Michael Oher could be considered responsible for the disadvantages he had to contend with.

If you are reading this book, you have a skill millions of people in the world, particularly women, have not had the privilege of learning. If you had the chance to go to school, to live in a residence of some sort with one or more parents nurturing you and loving you, you have had opportunities many in the world cannot even imagine. These are blessings from God, not of our own doing, and all blessings He has given us are meant to be shared. Before we blame those who are poor or at-risk, we need to remember we are not in the same situation largely because of factors not under our control.

We succumb to stereotypes and fear. Our tendency to carry stereotypes about those in need forms another barrier that prevents us from getting involved. Stereotypes can only be broken when we enter into the lives of people we don't know or understand. The misconceptions fall away as we realize the fullness of who a person is created to be, in God's image and able to reflect His beauty and grace. Diane Uy lives in Trenton, New Jersey, a city of 83,000 people, a fifth of whom live below the poverty level. She believes that a big reason people carry misconceptions about the inner city and the people who live there is because they haven't been there themselves. "Most people who live in the inner city are not criminals. They are there for a multitude of reasons, including needing to find affordable housing and wanting to be near family," Diane says. "I also like to remember that all people, even the drug dealers and their families who we sometimes encounter, are multifaceted with positive character traits and friendly personalities, even while they are engaged in illegal activities."

Diane tells the story of one gangbanger she met while working in the psychiatric ward of a local hospital; the kids who ended up there were often gang members in danger of their lives. One of these boys was the "enforcer of the gang, he was supposed to be the tough one, but he would talk about his teddy bear and how he would always sleep with it at night. That made me realize that inside that tough exterior was a little boy needing to be cared for," Diane says.

Tonya Herman, the missional mom from Compton, California, experienced the same deepening in her understanding of the people she met in her community. "When you see a kid and watch him become that gangbanger over time, he is not just a faceless monster. He is a person you know and love and grieve for. He has a mom and a grandmother and maybe even a child. As you love the poor, you see them for the people God created them to be rather than as black-and-white stereotypes," Tonya says. Missional moms do not succumb to stereotypes of those who are poor and downtrodden because they have had enough personal experience to know the individuals behind the labels society often gives them.

We desire safety for ourselves and especially for our children. We live in a time when the safety of our children is of paramount importance. In one Connecticut town, the mayor agreed to chop down three hickory trees after a woman worried a stray nut might find its way into her new swimming pool, "where her nut-allergic grandson occasionally swam."[7] It seems unthinkable to us to put ourselves or our kids in any situation in which they could experience harm, especially physical harm. And since ministering to those God wants us to reach can involve going to places seen as dangerous or risky, most moms would not actively choose either to bring her kids to such places or to go there herself.

But living in fear contradicts the Christ-follower's calling to live by faith. When we try to delineate what we will and will not do for God, for the purpose of protecting our children or ourselves, we dictate the terms of our faith journey instead of obeying God's mandates for us. "God, I will follow You, so long as I don't have to go to that part of town and meet those kinds of people" is not the spirit of obedience to God's call that He desires from us. "God, I don't want to do anything to put my children at risk" does not reflect an attitude of trust in the provision of God. In contrast, by faith Abraham was willing to sacrifice his own son in order to demonstrate his obedience to God. And God himself was willing to sacrifice His own Son to save us all. As excruciatingly hard as it is even to write or say these words, we must be willing to lay down our own lives and lay down our children before God, putting Him in the highest place. God offers salvation to us freely, but there is a cost to our discipleship. Given what God has more than willingly paid for our sakes and souls, we must similarly be willing to offer our lives in return.

This does not mean we willfully endanger or unwisely put our children or ourselves at risk. But it means that we don't shelter our families from experiencing and witnessing the challenging parts of the world we live in. When we spend all of our days in well-manicured communities that do not display a hint of the pain and suffering of this world, raising our children in neighborhoods where the most striking things they ever see are the growing sizes of McMansions on the street, we are not raising them in a world that fully reflects reality.

Missional moms come to terms with the challenge of letting go of fears as they seek to serve and love those in need. "We have taught our kids that God's protection is not a guarantee that nothing will happen to us," says Compton's Tonya Herman, a mother who has known danger up close and firsthand. Two years ago a shooting happened right outside her house. Her family had just gone to bed when a bullet lodged in the frame of their living room window, an inch from the glass. What Tonya took away from that incident was not that her family was in danger but quite the opposite: "I could see how God had protected us. If that bullet had come just an inch closer to the window, if our kids had still been in the living room, in all these ways He showed His protection," Tonya says. "If one of my children would ever be taken, of course I would be devastated. But when we experienced that bullet, it only strengthened my faith in God's provision. Sometimes Christians say, 'we're sold out to Christ,' but then we tell Him we won't live in certain areas. That's not really being sold out to Christ, then."

Tonya's experience was unusual; most missional moms who live or regularly work in what seem to be dangerous areas will tell you that the stereotypes portrayed in the media make these neighborhoods appear worse than they really are. The dangers may be real and present, but the media can exacerbate negative perceptions and create more fear than is necessary. Kirsten Strand says, "We were prepared for any negative situation before we moved to East Aurora. I thought I would feel a lot more scared walking through our neighborhood. But now I don't have any fear in living here. There have been huge upsides, in how much our kids play with other kids, or in how we hang out in the summertime around the grill with our neighbors. We were prepared for every and any negative thing that could have happened, but, at least so far, it hasn't been like that at all."

SO MANY UPSIDES . . .

Kirsten mentioned the word "upside," and the positive benefits seem countless, according to other missional moms serving the less fortunate despite risks or challenges. One "upside" is that spending time with "the least of these" shows us the fallacy of the cultural values of consumerism, materialism, and achievement orientation. These false paths to success or gratification begin to lose their attractiveness as the missional mom discovers the true joy and fulfillment that come from opening her heart to those whom society has largely forgotten or ignored. "One of the problems of living in wealthy neighborhoods is parents feeling that they need to expose their children to many activities at a young age," says Diane Uy. "There is much less of this in the inner city. It is easier for us to avoid materialism and competition when we live in a poorer neighborhood."

One recurrent theme of missional moms who have dedicated themselves to serving the most needy is, "You see the face of Jesus in the poor." The first time Katy White, who is now a physician from Paramount, California, took a trip to Mexico after college and worked in its garbage dumps as a student nurse, she saw "so much of Jesus in the poor, in their faith, in how they relied on Jesus for everything. For me, it was a much fuller picture of the gospel. I realized I have as much to learn from people who are poor as they have from me."

What comes through so clearly in regard to the Tuohy family's relationship with Michael Oher is the reciprocal nature of the blessings. It's amazing how much those we might aim to serve actually change us in the end. Serving and loving those who are the "least of these" is not intended to be a rescue operation in which those who have been given more resources enter into the lives of those who are poor or under-resourced and take all their problems away. Rather, what missional moms discover is how much, ultimately, they are the ones changed for the better. "Building relationships with people in poverty will show you a different side of the kingdom that you don't have," Katy says. "We need the people of the Comptons of the world as much as they need us. I see how much more I need Jesus when I see their need and brokenness and recognize my own."

"When we began Breakthrough, we didn't know much about homelessness and poverty," executive director Arloa Sutter says. "We just wanted to help people. What we didn't realize was that we would be getting into a journey in which we would be the ones who would learn and benefit so much."

HOW TO BEGIN LOVING
"THE LEAST OF THESE" IN YOUR LIFE

If you want to begin serving those in need, experienced missional moms suggest some practical ways to get involved.

1. Breakthrough's Arloa Sutter recommends pinpointing where your interests already lie and beginning there. For example, if you are already giving to a particular cause or volunteering, ask yourself whether you could take your involvement to the next step. The more you invest in areas of natural passion and interest, the more likely you will stay involved long term. "If you have a cause, whether it's early childhood education or helping single moms or supporting groups that work to eradicate sex trafficking, find out who is already doing something for that cause and join with them," Arloa

says. "Look for where God is already at work, and join with what God is doing. A cause isn't something you take on by yourself."

2. Sometimes opportunities fall into our laps or across our radar. Remember how Shayne Moore was influenced by attending Bono's Heart of America event? Remember how Kirsten Strand's life was changed simply by driving west out of her wealthier suburb into the needy one next door? Sometimes God opens our eyes to people or situations we've seen every day without really noticing. If nothing that's already on your radar strikes a chord in you, take the time to educate yourself on issues happening around the world. The more you become aware of issues and needs, the easier it will be to identify a focal point. Richard Stearns writes, "For most of my life, I gave little thought to the circumstances of Christians in far-away countries—mostly out of ignorance about their plight."[8] Yet now Stearns leads a global ministry and travels all over the world to determine how World Vision can serve those in great need. His journey from being the CEO of a luxury goods company to the head of World Vision began when he started to let his heart be touched and changed by the needs around him.

3. Take it step by step. No one has saved a city by herself or done so overnight. The day I met Arloa Sutter at the Breakthrough headquarters and toured the men's shelter, it was inspiring to see all the different activities going on—the food pantry, job and computer training, daily devotionals, just to name a few. Breakthrough has two shelters that serve a thousand homeless people each year, and it's easy to think, "How could I ever do something like this?" But Breakthrough did not happen overnight. The ministry as it operates today emerged over eighteen years of faithful, small steps by Arloa and many others. God did not show Arloa the big picture of what Breakthrough would become right from the start, and she still can't see the end result because there is always "the next thing to do. God keeps expanding the vision over time," Arloa says. In other words, our role is to be faithful in the little steps and let God handle the big-picture results.

"The poor you will always have with you," Jesus says; the work of loving the poor and the destitute will not go away this side of heaven. It is the calling of every Christian to faithfully love those in need—not once, not short term, but long term. Serving "the least of these" becomes a lifelong, ongoing part of our spiritual walk that brings believers to a new, rich experience of God. "It is exhausting to be driven by need," Arloa says, "because there will always be more needs than you can possibly meet. If instead you are led by the Spirit, God will lead you to the work you are called to do."

The work can be challenging, and it can be hard. But when we let our hearts be challenged and touched instead of shying away from the needs of the world that call for our involvement, amazing things can happen. Shayne Moore says, "We can't be insular anymore. We have to get down and dirty with people suffering. We have to have thick skin but yet keep our tender hearts."

Tender hearts are especially important as missional moms consider the subject of race. If loving our neighbors is about loving those vastly different from us, then loving our neighbors will come to a head for some people in the area of racial differences. We can learn much from missional moms who strive to be united and not divided in Christ.

CHAPTER SEVEN

The Missional Mom Is Third-Culture

Third culture is not just a trend
or a new thing but the heart of God.
DAVE GIBBONS

In 1974, a man named Bill Hybels launched a church in the northwestern suburbs of Chicago by relying on a simple truism: birds of a feather flock together. "We were all young, white, affluent, college-educated suburbanites, and we all understood each other. When we reached out to our friends, it became self-reinforcing," Hybels says.[1] The strategy succeeded: Willow Creek Community Church became one of the largest, most influential churches in the country. Today more than 23,000 people attend. Willow Creek's success sparked the birth of the megachurch movement and the rise of numerous churches in the U.S. reflecting a similar homogeneity among its membership. It seemed that adopting the strategy of encouraging people to befriend and worship with those similar to them was the right way to build a church.

But then something happened to Hybels. In 1999, he read *Divided by Faith: Evangelical Religion and the Problem of Race in America* by Michael Emerson, which noted that evangelical Christians had fewer minority acquaintances than non-Christians. Emerson concluded that evangelicalism was actually contributing to the "racial fragmentation of American society" rather than forming a bridge to bring people together. Reading this book shook Hybels to the core. He says, "I went from thinking 'I don't have a race problem' to 'There's a huge problem in our world that I need to be a part of resolving.'"[2]

As a result of Hybels's epiphany and subsequent changes made by the leadership at Willow Creek, the church has moved from being 2 percent ethnically diverse to being 20 percent diverse in seven years, a striking change. "I've actually come to believe that the extent to which we just worship with people who are like us, our worship is diminished. I really do think the church is enriched by its diversity," Hybels says. "When you have unity amongst that kind of diversity, that's something only God can do, and the world knows it."[3]

If your life is at all like mine, your friendships may have coalesced into a group of people who are largely similar. If you are a mom, your friends are probably mostly moms. If you are Caucasian, you may find your friendships are largely with other Caucasians, or if you're black, Asian, or Hispanic, you may notice your friendships also run along similar ethnic or racial lines. Or your relationships may largely be with those who share your educational or socioeconomic status. Life is so busy and demanding it's hard to maintain relationships with anyone at all, and so we tend to default to investing time only with those with whom the friendships come easily, those who make us feel the most comfortable.

What Bill Hybels learned—and what I've learned from missional moms who have intentionally pursued friendships with others radically different from themselves—is the great blessing and benefit that grows out of building diverse relationships. And of the many ways people vary from one another, our generation probably perceives one of the most profound differences to be in the area of race.

ONE MOM'S TRANSFORMATION

One of the points we gleaned from the parable of the Good Samaritan was that God wants us to love those who are different from us. More specifically, the parable of the Good Samaritan also celebrates a radical crossing of ethnic lines. God commands this kind of love from His people—a love that pushes against the boundaries of what might be comfortable and easy and strives to show love across any established barriers. When the world sees Christians who actively seek friendships across relational divides, we become a wonderful witness to what the love of Christ can do to build bridges between people.

Take, for instance, the story of Laura Goetsch, the mom of a four-year-old girl and twin toddler daughters. Laura's story tells of her gradual transformation from someone who rarely thought about issues related to race and culture to someone who actively pursued relationships across the divisions of ethnicity and culture.

Although Laura grew up with Asian-American friends in high school and an Asian-American roommate in college, it was not until after she graduated that she was challenged to truly understand what racial differences meant. At a training conference Laura attended, "A speaker said, 'If you are a white American, it makes a difference that you are in the majority culture; it makes a difference how you experience life,'" Laura says. "A lightbulb went on in my head. I realized I had made assumptions with my nonwhite friends, that the way I thought and did things was the way they thought and did things."

Laura suddenly saw her relationship with a former Asian-

American roommate in a whole new way. "I'd assumed that the very direct, upfront way I spoke to her was the way Lydia would communicate with me. In hindsight, I realized her way was actually much more indirect so that she wouldn't be shaming me. I had completely missed the cues she had been giving me about what she thought and wanted because I assumed we communicated the same way," Laura says.

Laura's experience in the training session opened her eyes to how much she had to learn about those from a different racial background, and she took the initiative to do something about it. Never having had a close African-American friend, she prayed, "Lord, I have no clue how to grow in this area. You have to help me." And God provided. Laura's next roommate was an African-American graduate student. "Growing in cross-racial understanding was the next step in my spiritual growth," Laura says. "We had studied Revelation 7 in our training conference, the beauty of the vision when every tongue and tribe from every nation are together, and I realized how much culture matters, how much we need to both embrace our own culture but also embrace others as well."

Laura started devouring books about race such as *Divided By Faith* (the book that had opened Bill Hybels's eyes), as well as *Being White* by Doug Schaupp and Paula Harris, and *More Than Equals* by Spencer Perkins and Chris Rice. The more she read, the more she became aware that her experience was very different from the way nonwhites experienced life in America. "I never used to understand what racism was. I never had experienced it. Then someone reminded me, 'You're white. You're part of the majority culture.' I had lived twenty-two years not realizing this fact."

Laura began to explore her own cultural background as well. "I discovered that even as a white person, I have a distinct cultural background. I am northern European, midwestern, college-educated at a Big Ten school. These elements inform my culture. It explains why I feel comfortable in Holland and Germany but not

The Missional Mom

so much in Italy. I started understanding my own cultural influences so much better."

Perhaps the most striking thing that helped Laura understand racial differences occurred right after she married and moved to Cleveland, where her husband worked. Laura says, "After a year-long search, we decided to go to an almost entirely black church. We were the only white faces in a sanctuary that seated eight hundred. At first I thought, 'This is too far out of my comfort zone. This is a totally different world. I'm not ready for this.' But the more we kept searching, the more we felt this church was to be our home."

The experience, Laura says, "was such a huge blessing. It was challenging at first; it was the first time I had ever been in the minority for a prolonged period. I grew so much in my understanding of what it means to be in the minority, how tiring it can be to have to understand the dominant culture and explain yourself or adjust. We grew in our understanding of African-American culture. We grew spiritually, too; there is so much understanding of the sweetness of Jesus in the black culture, and I grew to desire that in my own relationship with Jesus."

Having had a taste of what Revelation 7 can look like this side of heaven, Laura continues to seek out cross-cultural relationships and push the boundaries beyond friendships of comfort.

WHY BE UNCOMFORTABLE?

Part of what makes Laura's story inspiring is her willingness to step out of her comfort zone. Avoiding discomfort is probably the main reason many of us shy away from friendships with those who are different from us. Let's take some time to understand why we crave comfort, and what God really means when He seems to be offering comfort to us in Scripture.

We crave Edenic comfort: When I read about what life in Eden was like before the fall, I think it sounds absolutely lovely. Adam and Eve are in perfect harmony with each other, with God, with all of nature. Beyond beautiful, the Garden did not exhibit even an ounce of pain or hardship, and so it's not hard to assume that life was certainly comfortable as a result, in every sense of the word. Who would want anything different?

All this changed, of course, with the fall. God laid down the terrible edicts, the ramifications of which remain with us today—enmity and conflicts between men and women, burdensome work and toil, childbirth pain, and, most finally, death—effects we strive to minimize or eliminate altogether in our daily lives. We seek after comfort, on some level, because there is a part of our heart and soul that still desires to be in that pre-fall, Edenic state. We all long to live without pain, hardship, or relational conflicts or challenges, surrounded by the beauty of God's creation and in perfect fellowship with Him.

Yet, if you look through Scripture from that point onward, you never see mention of Eden as the place to which God wants for us to return. Eden is only mentioned one more time outside of the book of Genesis, and it is clear as you see the scope of Scripture that Eden is no longer the goal. Instead, New Jerusalem as expressed in the book of Revelation is the vision toward which we are to strive. This vision from Revelation 7 that Laura referred to is a picture of tremendous diversity, as "a great multitude that no one could count, from every nation, tribe, people and language" stand before the heavenly throne (Revelation 7:9). In this new city, God redeems His creation by wiping away all "enmity" that had characterized much of the Genesis curse and replacing it with a holy unity. It is a picture of people united despite their differences, racial or otherwise, in praise and worship to God. This new city, and not an Edenic garden, is the vision to which God is calling His people. But achieving the dream of the New Jerusalem does not come without struggle or sacrifice. When the apostle John wrote, "God will wipe away every tear from their eyes" (Revelation 7:17 and 21:4), he implied that there would be tears of pain before they reached their final destination. You cannot get to New Jerusalem without experiencing pain and suffering along the way. In other words: do not expect the road to be comfortable.

The comfort that God does *offer.* We need to recognize that God does not promise us relational comfort with other people just as He does not promise physical or material comfort. If anything, following Christ will bring discomfort into our lives and relationships, just as it did for Jesus as He sought to spread His message of loving our neighbors—and by "neighbors" I am referring to those vastly different from us. And even if loving others is uncomfortable or even painful, Scripture teaches us another paradox of the Christian life: that comfort actually comes as we enter into the discomfort of others. As Paul writes in 2 Corinthians, "For just as the sufferings of Christ flow over into our lives, so also through Christ our comfort overflows . . . if we are comforted, it is for your comfort, which produces in you patient endurance of the same sufferings we suffer" (2 Corinthians 1:5–6).

In other words, the kind of the comfort God offers us is a *spiritual* comfort, and the purpose of that comfort is that we will offer the same comfort to others as we embrace their pains and sufferings. Comfort is not something we should pursue as a goal. It is not a material, physical, or even relational possession. Comfort is a *spiritual* gift God gives us, one with the missional purpose that we are to share it with others. As we share the comfort we've received, particularly with those who are different from us, we come closer to reflecting the vision of the New Jerusalem that God offers us in Revelation—not a garden, but a city teeming with humanity in all its brokenness and discomfort, yet ultimately a humanity redeemed by the life-giving work of Christ and united as one in collective praise and worship to God.

The Third-Culture Mentality. So, our call as followers of Christ is not to embrace comfort—materially, physically, or relationally—but to offer to others whatever comfort we possess by virtue of being daughters of the Most High and followers of Christ. Our call is to pursue the discomfort that comes from entering into relationships with those who are different from us, and since race is one of those significant barriers that separate people, it is a good place to start as we seek to expand our boundaries and welcome strangers into our lives.

Dave Gibbons, author of *The Monkey and the Fish*, has developed a concept called the Third-Culture mentality, meaning an attitude that welcomes and pursues others outside our comfort zone. Gibbons defines Third-Culture as "the mind-set and will to love, learn, and serve in any culture, even in the midst of pain and discomfort."[4] The phrase comes from the idea that a person's "first culture" is her primary cultural background and that "second culture" is the expression of those who are not comfortable with their own first culture. In contrast, a Third-Culture perspective embraces both first and second cultures; it is able to live in the midst of both and flexible enough to accept even more cultural contexts.

I asked Dave Gibbons what this means for the majority of American believers, who likely live and work in ethnically homogenous settings, for whom Third-Culture living and thinking is not natural or automatic. "It's definitely a work of the Holy Spirit! To ask people to enter into pain and suffering, eat foods they don't like, or hang out with people who make them uncomfortable, is countercultural," he says. When Gibbons himself felt God prompting him to live out his Third-Culture mentality with more intentionality, he and his family took the plunge by moving to Bangkok. "It starts with prayer," says Gibbons, "then someone must take the lead."

Third-Culture living might seem to us to be something ideal, but optional. However, Gibbons believes that avoiding the Third-Culture life has serious implications:

> The ramifications of not becoming Third-Culture are serious: we die spiritually. When we miss out on loving the other, we miss out on knowing what it is to love God. Then we are not fulfilling the purposes of why we're on this earth. Also, as we love others, we start a

The Missional Mom

journey of beauty. We see the different colors and nuances of who our God is, far beyond our greatest imagination.

For Dave Gibbons, one part of his journey to be a Third-Culture Christian led overseas. But you don't have to go to another country to follow a Third-Culture lifestyle. Instead, you can start by asking yourself how you might push the boundaries of your natural friendship circles. For those of us in America, pushing the race boundary is often the easiest way to begin a journey of transformation to becoming a Third-Culture Christian.

I don't live overseas or even in a particularly diverse neighborhood, but I felt convicted by Gibbons's challenge to think about my current circles of friendship. My church is largely ethnically homogeneous, with only a few African-Americans. I was saddened to realize I had rarely taken the time to connect with any of those African-Americans beyond the occasional "good morning." So at our next church event, when I spotted Jean in the parking lot, I stopped to introduce myself and to chat, and apologized for taking so long to meet her.

"That's okay," Jean said, with an air of resignation. "No one knows me around here." I felt a deep sense of sadness that here in my own church I'd had an opportunity to be more of a Third-Culture Christian, and I had been missing it all this time. As Jean and I got to know each other that day, we talked about being mothers, about Jesus, and about our different food preferences. We made plans to get together so I could learn how to cook a proper Southern gumbo. All this happened in one ten-minute conversation, and I left wishing I'd taken the time to connect with her earlier, as well as realizing how disconnected she had felt from the rest of the church because others had kept their distance, too.

"The ramifications of not being Third-Culture are serious: we die spiritually," Gibbons says. I find these extraordinarily challenging words. Yet how many times in your own spiritual life do you feel something is missing, that the spark of your earlier passion for Christ has died down over time? Perhaps the missing link is to pursue what we may be unintentionally or intentionally avoiding —a Third-Culture spirit—to take our Christian commitment to the next level. Today's missional moms are pursuing a Third-Culture mentality in their relationships out of a desire to obey God, particularly by crossing racial boundaries.

REAL-LIFE THIRD-CULTURE MOMS

Dana Gilbreath makes the effort to be a Third-Culture, missional mom. She and her husband, Ed, are African-Americans who live in a western suburb of Chicago. When they were trying to determine where to live, they looked for neighborhoods that reflected the diversity of God's kingdom. As a "military brat," Dana grew up around a variety of cultures. "I lived in communities with Filipino and Guamanian neighbors next door and a family from Holland across the street," Dana says. "I wanted my kids to live someplace where it was possible to have that kind of diversity." She also volunteers in the community as a Girl Scout troop leader, making an effort to invite girls from a variety of ethnic backgrounds to participate. "Most of the troops in this area are 99 percent white," she says. "Ours is the most diverse troop around. We have girls from every background—Filipino, Cambodian, Chinese, Mexican, African-American, Caucasian—and we educate one another about our cultures."

As a result of Dana's proactive efforts to keep connected with people from different ethnic backgrounds, she has had opportunities to discuss questions about race with other moms who are Girl Scout troop leaders, which has led to greater understanding on all sides of their respective differences. "I have known the women I do Girl Scouts with for five years. I'm the only black leader," Dana says. "We go on a camping trip every year, and every year we get into a discussion about race. They always have questions for me, and they are comfortable asking me because they know I will be open and understanding."

On one of these trips, a white high school teacher asked Dana, "The black kids in my class are always so loud. Why is it that black kids are always so loud?" Although a question like this could have made Dana uncomfortable, she gave her friend the benefit of the doubt that she truly desired to understand. Dana answered, "Part of the reason is very much cultural. African-Americans have been silenced for so long, and our voices have not always been heard, so we tend to speak louder in order to be heard, in all circumstances." As the only black person in her friendship groups, Dana often plays the role of ambassador. She says, "I can give my friends a perspective to help them understand my cultural background, if they are open to talking and learning more about it. And I've learned from them, too. Even when the discussions are challenging, these interactions go beneath just casual, everyday interactions, and they help our friendships grow much deeper."

Katy White, my college friend who works as a physician in an inner-city clinic, is a Caucasian woman whose horizons grew beyond her own cultural background after she spent a year working with impoverished communities in Mexico. "I learned Spanish, and I gained a love for Spanish-speaking people, for their culture, to the point that I knew I was being called to work with them," Katy says. "I began to understand that, in my previously very white world, I had never really built relationships with others who were different from me, particularly with African-Americans and Latino people, when God really wants for us to be involved in reconciling relationships."

At her church, Katy now prefers attending the noontime service, where a larger percentage of those who attend are from the working class, or are poor, and the demographics are more ethnically diverse. Interestingly, the discomfort she has begun to experience as a result of pursuing relationships with those who are different has come from a surprising source: from other Caucasians. "People sometimes make comments to my husband, Bill, who is a pastor at our church. They say, 'Why doesn't Katy like white people? She just wants to spend time with other races.' But I have to make those intentional choices *not* to spend time only with people like me, which would be so much easier to do," Katy explains.

Some missional moms become Third-Culture by taking the radical step of adopting a child from another cultural background. Adopting a child into your family, particularly one from an ethnic background other than your own, is a lifelong, life-changing way to immerse your family in Third-Culture living and loving.

Jennifer Grant is a columnist for the *Chicago Tribune* and the mother of four children. Her youngest, Mia, is adopted. Mia was born in Guatemala and is of Mayan descent, and having Mia as a part of Jennifer's family has helped everyone become more aware of issues of race. "We've had a lot of comments about her race, especially when she first came home," Jennifer says. "Once when I was in line at the post office, with all four of my children, a man turned around and said to us, 'One of them doesn't match.' I get mad now when I see how few images of Latino people appear in mainstream media. Having a daughter 'of color' certainly sensitizes me."

Not only has having Mia as a part of her family increased Jennifer's cultural sensitivity, but it has also raised the awareness of Mia's siblings. Jennifer says of her daughter Isabel, "When we are in a place with more people of color, such as in the city, or at a hotel pool on vacation, I notice that Isabel is immediately drawn toward the kids of color. At school, she has a completely mixed group of friends. Having a sister of color has made my kids very comfortable with people of color in general." When parents embrace a child of a different ethnicity as their own, the message for other siblings in the house is clear: this is a family for whom love knows no racial boundaries. That is Third-Culture living.

WHY BEING THIRD-CULTURE
IS IMPORTANT FOR YOUR KIDS

As in Jennifer's family, Third-Culture living has significant impact on your children, especially in shaping their attitudes and perspectives on race. In their fascinating book *Nurture Shock*, researchers Po Bronson and Ashley Merryman outlined key findings about parenting and the topic of race. Infants even as young as six months old notice differences in skin color and stare longer at photographs of people of a race different from their own. Before long, children begin to make value judgments about those racial differences. When a group of three-year-old white children were given opportunities to choose photographs of other children they'd like to pick for a friend, 86 percent chose someone of their own race. That means by age three, the children had already categorized people by race and developed racial preferences.

Bronson and Merryman also referenced a 2007 study in the *Journal of Marriage and Family*, which reported that out of 17,000 families with a kindergartner, 75 percent of the white families surveyed "almost never talk about race."[5]

If most families with young children don't talk about race, and yet children as young as three years old begin to make qualifications in their minds that their best friends should be those who look most like them, then we can see how easy it is for children to grow into adults who shy away from friendship with people of a different racial background. What I found most alarming in Bronson's and Merryman's research was how quickly the window can shut for children as they try to make sense of the diversity they see. In one experiment to determine when kids' attitudes toward race are more amenable to change, a class of first-graders was divided into groups of six kids, with each group being racially diverse. These groups met for eight weeks, twice a week, with each child taking a turn teaching a lesson to the other children. Then, the children were observed on the playground, to see if the group interactions would lead to more cross-racial social interaction. The result? "Having been in the cross-race study groups led to significant cross-race play."[6] But this was only true for first-graders! Once the children became third-graders, the cross-racial study groups had no impact on increasing cross-race play. The implication is that by the time parents might feel it is appropriate to begin conversations about race, "the developmental window has already closed."

Missional moms talk to their kids about race, early and often. They strive to build cross-racial friendships with other families so their kids learn early that those racially different from them are not to be feared or avoided but befriended and understood. The more we make it a habit to reach out and develop cross-racial relationships, even if it may feel uncomfortable, the more our children's generation will begin to see racial differences as a nonissue. When our children see racial discrimination or prejudices, they will be sensitized to it.

Katy White's eleven-year-old son Timothy recently brought a friend, Greg, to a church youth group event. Later he found out that Greg did not have a good time. Timothy thought the reason could have been because his friend was the only Asian-American boy there, as the youth group comprises predominately Hispanic, Caucasian, and African-American children. "Another child was hounding Greg with questions and comments that were probably offensive and inappropriate. We were so disappointed," Katy says. "But we used the opportunity to talk about how Greg might have felt, and we shared with Timothy about how upset we were that Greg was treated that way. Before bedtime that night, Timothy said, 'I'm happy to be who I am, but tonight I wished I were Asian too.' I was so thankful to hear his sensitivity and to see his soft heart for his friend."

THE GREAT PARADOX

Improving race relations is one of the critical issues facing our country, and particularly facing the church. As a result of our

The Missional Mom

country's unique history and immigration patterns, the U.S.'s growing diversity gives us potential for conflicts, yes, but also for cross-racial understanding. The Christian community can make so much impact and serve as an incredible witness to demonstrate how powerful the love of Christ really is, especially as Christians build bridges across racial lines.

As you try to expand your horizons to include Third-Culture relationships, begin by examining what unexamined prejudices might be keeping you from building bridges with those different from you. For example, I am an Asian-American, specifically a second-generation Korean-American. I don't know if learning this changes your perception of me or whether it changes how you view the book, but if it does, it might be useful to think about why the information matters to you and in general to gain a greater understanding of the impressions we have of people from other ethnic backgrounds. No matter what our heritage, we can learn a great deal from others if we take initiative, step out of our comfort zone, and seek to build relationships with those who are unlike us.

As mothers we have an opportunity for tremendous influence in helping the church become a place reflecting God's love that knows no bounds. Mothers who want to become more Third-Culture in their personal friendships have a wonderful context for building bridges with others, through sharing their motherhood experiences. What mother, her race or ethnicity aside, can't relate to the challenges of raising children, of trying to get them to sleep or to eat or to play nicely with other children? These are universal challenges, and when mothers connect with other mothers, they easily create connections through their shared experiences.

As in so many other critical points during the history of the church, mothers can make a significant difference. We can further the church's progress in loving those from different cultural backgrounds, as we build relationships with other mothers and foster relationships among our children, relationships that ultimately help us recognize how similar we all really are. This is the great paradox of pursuing Third-Culture living: for all the emphasis we place on the differences between people, as we come together we discover there is much more that unites us than divides us.

CHAPTER EIGHT

The Missional Mom
Creates
Missional Families

What will make family exciting,
what will make it worthy of our commitment
and take us through the dry times,
is our common commitment to
a mission bigger than our family.

RODNEY CLAPP

As any mother who spends a part of her day working in a field of employment knows, you are only as good as your babysitter. Until recently, that critical position in our household was held by a wonderful young man named Phil Pearson, a Wheaton College student we met at the beginning of his sophomore year who cared for our boys several afternoons a week until he graduated this past spring. Many times I have only been able to conduct interviews or research because Phil was in my house, skill-fully watching over my three little boys and giving me time to pursue the mission of writing.

Last January, Phil came at his usual time in the afternoon, and I could tell from his face that something was wrong. "I have something I need to tell you," he said. "We just found out that my mom has leukemia."

Phil's mother, Mary, had been diagnosed with a rare form of blood cancer called acute lymphocytic leukemia. A disease more common in children, it was made difficult to treat by the fact that Mary was an adult, and she began her battle right away with an aggressive course of chemotherapy. Our whole family began to follow Mary's situation with great concern. Even though we had never met, I felt connected to this other mother, whose own son was caring for my sons. We rejoiced with Phil when it looked as though the cancer had gone into remission. We shed tears of sorrow when her leukemia returned this past fall, when in November she was given only four-to-six weeks to live. With courage and tremendous heart, Mary outlasted those predictions about her life expectancy until exactly one week after Phil graduated from college in May, when she passed away.

Although Mary is no longer present on this earth, this devoted mother left behind numerous legacies reflecting her devotion to family and to the God she so faithfully served. Although I never met Mary, I can tell you a great deal about her values and her family culture by what I see in Phil—by the way he carries him-self, by his competence with our boys, by his good judgment, and by his lack of any semblance of self-entitlement. I can tell he under-stands the value of a dollar; I know he will be a wonderful dad some day, and I was witness to his unwavering faith in Jesus, a faith reflected in the way both of his parents so bravely dealt with the diagnosis and treatment of Mary's cancer. Even though I will not meet this inspiring woman this side of heaven, Mary's legacy lives on through her children and through a blog journal that contin-

The Missional Mom

ues to minister to me and others. Mary Pearson may never have referred to herself in these terms, but she was very much a missional mom.[1]

We've thoroughly established how many aspects of the culture we live in run counter to God's intent for us and about how missional moms strive instead to live in a manner worthy of the gospel. We turn now to how missional moms become culture shapers, how they can actually help to change the culture and not just live counter to it. Mary Pearson's example suggests a significant way moms can have lasting impact: through the culture they create in their families.

CULTURE CHANNELS

A number of years ago, I worked on the staff of a little-known but well-respected magazine for young Christian leaders who desired to have meaningful impact in the cultural sphere they inhabited. Led by editor Andy Crouch, *re:generation quarterly* regularly professed that there are seven key channels through which cultural impact occurs:

- Politics/government
- Arts and entertainment
- The media
- The academy (education)
- The professions (business, medicine, law)
- The church and parachurch
- The home

One of those cultural channels is a place where mothers wield an enormous amount of influence—the home. Many of us will also participate in channels outside the home, but as moms we all have the potential to make a significant cultural mark on the world by the difference we make in our families' lives.

A majority of the missional moms I've met come from homes with parents who were particularly missional as well. Therefore, being a missional mom is likely the most significant way to help your own children become missional in their lives. As you create a family culture that exudes mission-driven values, your children will begin to accept those values and may even transmit them to their own children one day. It is no exaggeration to say that being missional today could resonate for generation after generation.

We have already established that many adults fall away from faith in God, despite early conversion moments. This trend of departure from the established church is especially noticeable these days among young adults. According to a 2006 Barna Group study, 60 percent of twenty-somethings who were active in the Christian faith in their teenage years are no longer regularly attending church, praying, or reading the Bible.[2] In some studies, evangelical teens are depicted as *more* likely than non-Christian peers to have lost their virginity.[3] Despite their efforts, Christian parents seem more ineffective than ever at helping their children embrace an authentic Christianity that lasts through the tumults and trials of young adult life.

Ken Fong is the senior pastor of Evergreen Baptist Church of Los Angeles, a missional, multiethnic church in Rosemead, California. He believes that part of the problem stems from parents who desire their children to be compliant and obedient, rather than helping them to have either a true picture of Jesus or of the mission he has given us all. Fong says:

> When most of what we expect is compliance, then we never know how deeply our children have embraced God's gospel as their own . . . we just want to see that they're apparently meeting our (and God's) expectations . . . Without realizing it, the gospel that we give our children isn't a powerful gospel because it doesn't have to be. So that limp gospel is relatively easy to reject and walk away from.[4]

In contrast, missional family culture helps make the Christian faith real and tangible. For children, Christianity no longer becomes just an exercise in saying the right things about Jesus or demonstrating blind obedience. Instead, their faith comes to life as they see their parents pursue the goal of realizing the kingdom of God on earth. The more that children can participate with their parents in fulfilling God's mission in the world, the more likely they will grasp that Christianity actually makes a difference in a believer's life. Although no parent is truly in control of their children's futures, they do have enormous influence over the attitudes, beliefs, and practices their children will exhibit in their adult lives. What are some ways missional parents can create a family culture that demonstrates a vibrant faith that matters?

HOW MISSIONAL MOMS
CREATE MISSIONAL FAMILIES

Becoming missional does not just happen naturally, because being missional often involves acting against dominant cultural values. So it takes initiative and proactive choices to be missional yourself and to pass the same lifestyle to your children. Here are some key ways today's missional moms strive to incorporate missional living in their families.

They resist materialism. No one denies that strong cultural forces of consumerism and materialism dominate our country. Missional moms take practical and intentional steps to reduce the effects of these forces in their own spending and ownership choices. They strongly consider the questions "Do I *want* this?" and "Do I *need* this?" when making purchases and pass on that practice to their children.

Our tendency to covet what we do not have makes this much harder. Missional moms strive to find ways to paint a picture of reality for their children that emphasizes how much they have in contrast to what they lack. "We can have such a warped view of the world because we are surrounded by so much abundance," says Tonya Herman of Compton. "Compared with the kids in our community, my kids are wealthy. But what we've learned from those children in poverty is how they have a generosity that comes from experiencing adversity."

Missional moms intentionally shape their children's view of the world to help them build this right perspective of appreciating the blessings and bounty of their lives. These moms may limit their children's exposure to commercials, catalogs, toy stores, and other situations that might lead the children to foster a mind-set of coveting what other kids have. Of course, there is no way to remove these influences completely, but if parents are mindful of the messages their children are receiving from society, they can reduce the number of those messages that say "Buy!" and "Spend!" and "You must have this!" Limiting the temptation to covet can go a long way toward helping them stand firm against the temptation to put hope in material things.[5]

We get catalogs at our house—lots and lots of catalogs! Once you buy a few things online or from a mail-order company, marketers quickly resell the names and addresses and other companies discover there are children in the house. Every month, we receive catalogs from toy companies I've never even heard of, and I used to leave them around without thinking about it. Then I realized my boys would pore through the catalogs and start making a mental list—creating an "I wish I could have that!" perspective. Now I automatically recycle all toy magazines unless I am looking for something specific for one of my kids, and even then I hide them!

We also spend time talking with our boys about marketing strategies that companies use to persuade us to buy their products. Since today's businesses spend more than fifteen billion dollars every year to target children, we have to help our kids discern the difference between truth and marketing jargon. My boys enjoy playing with cars, as many boys do, and one day I heard my eldest

The Missional Mom

say to his brother, "I'm going to get a BMW someday. It is the ultimate driving machine!" That gave me a good opportunity to discuss how marketers craft their words and to dissect why a slogan can't be taken literally. Now my kids will even catch me if I seem to be longing over some miracle house product that promises to whisk away all my dirt and dust and problems. "You can't believe what you see in an advertisement, Mom!" I'll hear them say. It doesn't take long for kids to start helping the parents battle materialism once they are shown the way!

Missional moms constantly find ways to demonstrate generosity. There is no better antidote to materialism than to be generous and to encourage our children to give freely. Missional moms involve their children in giving. It may take more time to create opportunities for kids to actively participate in giving, but the more they give, the more they too will embrace the missional value of open-handed generosity.

Your family might sponsor a child through Compassion International or World Vision, choosing together to sacrifice something in order to afford the monthly cost. This might mean giving up cable television, staying home instead of eating out once a month, or asking relatives to give your kids money to donate instead of traditional birthday gifts. You can help alleviate poverty by using websites such as www.kiva.org, which provides microlending opportunities for impoverished people, who take those donations and build a way of sustenance for themselves and their families. Or check out www.heifer.org to purchase livestock that can help a family both feed themselves and raise animals that can be sold in the marketplace. Whatever way you choose to bless the world, make it a family decision so your children can take ownership of the idea and embrace it as their own.

To celebrate the recent birthday of her daughter Caris, Katy White suggested the family host a World Vision party. Caris loved the idea and helped make all the plans. "Instead of gifts, people brought $10, or what they could, to the party," explains Katy.

"During the party they chose gifts through the World Vision catalog. We ended up getting a goat and two chickens for people in developing countries with the $125 people brought." Katy and her husband gave another $60 to pay for ten ducks, one in honor of each child who attended the party. "It was an awesome experience for us all," Katy reports. "The other kids were really excited about it, too. Even kids who couldn't come donated for the cause!"

Children can be involved in many practical demonstrations of generosity and love for those in need. "We are always trying to ask our kids to think about the question, 'How can we help people?'" says Minhee Cho, co-founder of One Day's Wages (www onedayswages. org), a grassroots organization dedicated to ending extreme global poverty. "With children, you can start with small things," says Minhee. "A few years ago, a friend of mine started a brown bag project with kids as a way to help the homeless. We prepared bags that had socks, water, granola bars, and scarves, and then we put them in our cars to give away whenever we would see someone homeless." Minhee says the project opened up conversations with her kids about how people become homeless and how to help them. Her children became aware of this segment of society that can often be ignored.

That initial project sparked the kids' desire to do more. So Minhee took the idea to the moms' ministry at Quest Church in Seattle, where her husband, Eugene, is the pastor. Before long ten women had gathered donations and supplies to create two hundred brown bags, which were then sold to the congregation so members of the church family could also have something tangible in their cars to give to the homeless people they encountered. Children in the church helped assemble the bags and wrote notes of encouragement to put inside. The project became both a way to raise more money to serve the needs of others and a way to spread the idea of caring for the needs of the homeless. When children have the chance to use their skills and talents to serve, they remember those tangible moments, which helps to build a spirit of generosity and tenderness toward those in need. Giving becomes a powerful antidote to combat the attitudes and behaviors of self-entitlement and self-indulgence that come when children are not encouraged to think beyond their own needs and desires.

Missional moms do not shield their children from the realities of life. We've seen already the many ways missional moms have not sat idly by in the face of the world's enormous needs. They pass on to their children a similar awareness of what is happening in the world, keeping them engaged and involved. Sometimes we mothers want to protect our children from knowing too much about the pain and sadness, but the sooner we help them gain an understanding of global issues, the sooner they can contribute their efforts to do something about it.

You will remember Patsy Chavarria, the missional mom who evangelizes others by empathizing with their struggles and sharing her own pain. Patsy struck a good balance in involving her children in the work she was doing in the city of Compton through her church, Emmanuel Reformed Church (ERC). Every year, ERC conducts transformation and renewal projects in Compton, and Patsy is one of the "lieutenants" who lead a team of people to re-do a house, for example. Initially, Patsy pushed her kids to accompany her, but then she realized that "this is my passion, but it might not be their passion. So I told them I wouldn't require them to come anymore." Patsy kept serving, keeping her family informed about what she and the rest of the church were doing in Compton, and the reasons for their efforts in that needy community.

One year her daughter Charli decided to come with Patsy again, to help out in the rehabilitation of a Compton resident's house. "Charli was so moved by the experience that she said she wants to come to every Compton project after this," Patsy says. "She gave up her entire spring break this year and came with me to work twelve-hour days because now she sees that she can be a blessing to others." One can easily imagine that as Charli continues to use her talents and gifts to serve, she will be building habits of generosity and of caring for the needs of others that can last a lifetime.

While ONE Campaign activist and "global soccer mom" Shayne Moore was in Zambia on her missions trip in 2009, she posted photos depicting the realities she encountered there. During her trip, unbeknownst to Shayne, her daughter, Greta, printed the photos to share with her fifth-grade class at school, ending with a photo of a little Zambian girl, confident and smiling. Greta wrote on that last page, "Everybody can make a difference in the world no matter how small you are." Shayne was amazed to see how, even while she was still away, her daughter understood the need to be aware of the needs of others and already saw that she could be a part of the solution. "The whole trip was worth that moment," Shayne says.

Keeping your kids informed does not just have to do with global needs; it can can happen in smaller ways, too, such as explaining to your children what "fair trade coffee" means and having them help you find some in the store or telling them about global warming and explaining how wasting energy affects the polar bears they love so much.[6] The more you grow in your own awareness, the more you can pass on what you learn. Life is full of thousands of teachable moments when a mom can transmit missional values to her children. As children see the intentionality behind their parents' life choices, small and big, they will learn habits of thinking and acting that may one day be reflected in their own missional lives.

Missional moms make a regular practice of hospitality. Back in my days of campus ministry, I kept an open-door policy for my apartment so students could constantly be coming and going. No one ever called beforehand; students would just come and hang out, and we'd share into the wee hours, studying, laughing, talking, sometimes crying, and just doing life together in numerous ways. But once I'd married and had kids, I found myself more and more inclined to withdraw into our own house and lives. As much as I love my kids, being with them all day would drain my introverted self, and it was difficult to think about opening the doors of our house to anyone else. Plus, my house was frequently a mess. Then when homeschooling became a part of our agenda, there was even less time and energy to be hospitable. Yet something seemed missing in our lives as a result.

"Why is it that so many Christian households remain firmly shut to the outsider? Why is it that we find it so hard to open up our homes?" ask missional church leaders Alan and Debra Hirsch. "Most of us will serve at the church, give some money to the poor, and perhaps even go out on mission trips, but when it comes down to bringing that mission 'home,' we flatly refuse. More than that, we see it as our personal space that ought not be intruded upon. After all, isn't the home the domain of the family? And isn't my family the safe haven for those I am responsible for?"[7]

But missional moms challenged me with their radical expressions of hospitality, with their openness to more than just friends and acquaintances, with their welcoming of the stranger into their homes and lives. Remember the three mothers from Southern California who were introduced in chapter 3? Rachel VerWys is quick to welcome strangers or invite a whole family from another country to stay with them indefinitely. Katy White had a troubled young woman stay with her family for a while, and Tonya Herman took in two brothers to be her godsons. Most of us can hardly fathom opening our homes to such a degree! Yet God has called all Christians to "practice hospitality," as Paul stated simply in the book of Romans. Hospitality is not an expression of Christian charity restricted to those who have a particular gift for it. Hospitality is not about having the perfectly clean house, the right style of place settings, or the proper gourmet menu to offer your guests. Hospitality is an invitation for others to join into our lives, no matter how messy our houses may be, figuratively or literally, for the purpose of sharing the blessings we have received from God. Hospitality provides an opportunity to show generosity, love, and grace, ideally toward those who are most in need.

Jennifer Jukanovich and her family demonstrated this quality of hospitality when they hosted weekly summer barbecues in their mixed-income Seattle neighborhood. Word quickly spread about the Jukanoviches' open dinners, and on average they would find thirty-five to fifty neighborhood kids in their backyard. Among their frequent visitors were gang members and other troubled youth who did not have people in their lives to show them care and concern. "It was such a blessing for us and for our kids," Jennifer says. "We got into all kinds of conversations about love, death, faith. Yes, it took time and resources, but it felt like such an amazing way to offer a safe haven to these kids who would otherwise be just wandering around on the street."

Jennifer and her family no longer live in Seattle; a year ago they sensed a call to serve "the least of these" with two other families in Rwanda. There they have created an organization that leveraged their prodigious business skills for the purpose of encouraging economic development among native Rwandan entrepreneurs.[8] But the Jukanovich family has continued to find ways to demonstrate hospitality, even as newcomers to a foreign land.

"While we no longer host weekly barbecues, our home has become a favorite neighborhood hangout," Jennifer says. "The highlight for me this year was hosting a Kwika Izina, which is a naming ceremony for our son we adopted in Rwanda. We had neighborhood children and their parents from the slums attend, as well as Rwandan businessmen and women, and 'mazungus,' or white people, all celebrating our son's arrival together. There were close to eighty people there, and it was unique to see so many people from different worlds together at one party, but that is what I love to do."

Missional moms consider radical expressions of hospitality, such as adoption. As Jennifer mentioned, the Jukanoviches welcomed a third child, two-year-old Rwandan Nathanael Niyonzima, into their family, to join their two daughters previously adopted from China, Lian and Anna.

Missional leader J.R. Briggs says, "The most radical hospitality expression that Christians can do is adoption. Radical hospitality is inviting people into your home for life, and adoption is the greatest expression of that. It is not for everyone, but at the same time, everyone should have a serious conversation about it with God and see what He says."

A recent *Christianity Today* article noted that since 2004, there has been a 40 percent decline in overseas adoptions by Americans.[9] Domestically, there are approximately 100,000 orphans, and Briggs notes that there are 350,000 churches in the U.S. "If just one family from every 3.5 churches in America decided they would adopt, the problem of orphans in the U.S. would be largely eliminated," Briggs says.

Briggs comes from a family committed to adoption; his brother and sister-in-law have recently returned from Ethiopia, where they became the parents of a six-year-old girl and her two-year-old brother. Briggs's sister-in-law Julie was a woman who experienced the call to adoption well before she had even met her husband. "I have been involved in orphan ministry since I was seventeen," Julie says. "Most of my travels took me to Russia to work with orphans at camps and orphanages. These trips gave me a deep desire to be a mother to orphans someday. I even told Alan before we got engaged that if he wanted to marry me, it meant adopting kids . . . We've decided to adopt *before* trying to have biological children because we really want our adopted children to know they were our plan all along."[10]

There is a wide spectrum of ways we can practice hospitality; not everyone is called to either domestic or overseas adoption, but we can all stretch the boundaries of how we currently exercise the spiritual discipline of hospitality. As with any spiritual discipline, the best way to turn it into a regular practice is to schedule it in. You might make an effort to have visitors in your house every week, for example, particularly those who are different from you and your family in some way. Maybe you will even take the radical challenge of remaining open to the possibility of welcoming others, long-term, into your home—through foster parenting, or temporary housing for homeless or immigrant families, or even adoption. You never know how God might change a life through your efforts—and change your life and your family's life in the process. Adoption, after all, is a metaphor for what God has done for each of us who calls herself a child of His. How better to express our understanding of this spiritual reality than to offer an orphan a chance of being enfolded into a family?

Missional moms help their families serve together. Missional activity is not meant to be accomplished in isolation, so serving together regularly is essential for missional families. "I see so clearly in Scripture that God calls us as families to serve Him, to follow Him, to love our neighbors," says Katy White. "So, as much as it is possible to involve the kids, involve them. Invite people into your home, bring your kids to the local food bank or whatever ministry you can do, talk about the call to love 'the least of these' at the dinner table."

The Newkirk family strives to live out missional service to others as a family. They live in Austin, Texas, and regularly organize the annual family mission trip for their church. This year they hosted a VBS program for low-income *colonias* in South Texas, a part of the U.S. that has the largest concentration of people living without basic services that most Americans take for granted—water, sewer systems, electricity, paved roads, and safe housing, for example.[11] Since the family is fluent in Spanish, they worked specifically with the preschoolers, and the Newkirk kids were integrally involved in the project. "My children are helping me prepare the lessons and the crafts, and they will help me teach," Marta Newkirk told me in the days before their trip. "Our children are growing up much like their parents, taking leadership responsibilities at young ages."

Upon their return from the missions trip, Marta reported that it had been a wonderful experience. She was especially blessed to learn of the impact her own family had on other families who were part of the experience. "Would you believe that two of the fourteen families gave testimonies saying that they were on this mission trip because in past summers they had watched how the Newkirks were so committed to going on the mission?" Marta was amazed—and gratified that her family could spread its missional focus. When families minister together, they inspire other families to do the same.

As children truly absorb missional thinking, they begin to reflect these values in their own choices. Marta's kids "regularly give out of their own money to missions efforts, like stoves for Ethopians, water filters for the Sudanese, Bibles for Native American reservations. They ask for more chores around the house so that they can give that money to missions offerings. They hardly ever buy anything for themselves with their earned money. They put that money into mission projects or buy gifts for those they consider to be in need."

As a typical suburban mom whose own children love to earn money in order to purchase the next Star Wars Lego figure on their list, I was humbled by the example of Marta's family and others whose children seemed to truly understand the call to serve and love. I wondered if starting to serve more as a family would help our boys more readily embrace these values. So last spring, I endeavored to include my older two boys, who were then seven and five, in service activities. I put them to work stuffing envelopes and affixing labels and stamps for our church's community health fair, which we were hosting in large part to reach children from lower-income neighborhoods near our church. Then my kids helped me deliver flyers door-to-door. Aside from the occasional crooked label or upside-down stamp, the boys were a big help. When they saw all the children who came to the fair from the neighborhood where we had passed out flyers, they came away with that simple but powerful idea: "Yes, I can make a difference."

Then our entire family, including our toddler and my

husband, went to the under-resourced neighborhood of East Garfield Park on the west side of Chicago to bring and serve a meal at Breakthrough Urban Ministries' shelter for homeless women, along with other volunteers from our church. It was the first time my kids had ever come into contact with people who are homeless, and it was also the first time they used their musical gifts for the purpose of serving rather than just performing. My eldest, a pianist, and my five-year-old, a violinist, played a duet and received an amazing response from the women at the shelter. "You boys have to come back and visit us again!" one said. They also enjoyed socializing with the shelter residents over lunch, and we hadn't been out the door for a minute before the boys were asking, "When can we go back?" I was just barely recovering from our brief time of service, and they already wanted to return.

We have a long way to go as a family as we learn to incorporate missional values in our daily life, but I have been stirred to see even on a small level how quickly children welcome these values if they are exposed to them. Sometimes I feel that the biggest stumbling block to our kids becoming more missional is me, the parent. It's hard to live sacrificially; to consistently serve those in need; to offer hospitality that requires a cost of time, energy, and loss of privacy; to think about taking orphans into a life that already feels so full. Yet these are exactly the ways God is calling us to live. Serving with my boys at Breakthrough taught me that children are the most open to the ideas of missional living, and as soon as we adults take up the mantle of missional living, it won't be long before the kids will follow, if not lead, our efforts.

CHAPTER NINE

The Missional Mom Is a Culture-Maker

The only way to change culture is to make more of it.
ANDY CROUCH

One of my favorite children's books is *Frindle*, written by Andrew Clements, about a fifth-grade boy named Nick Allen who wonders how words used in the English language become commonly accepted. "Who decides what words get to be in the dictionary?" he asks his teacher, the no-nonsense stickler Mrs. Granger. "You do, Nicholas," she replies, not realizing that by saying so, she has opened the door to Nick's own personal cultural revolution.

Nick, on a whim one day and without any premonition, calls a pen a "frindle." He has invented an entirely new word for this commonly used and known object, and what ensues is a hilarious and ultimately touching story about how one boy with a singular purpose can have worldwide cultural impact. I don't want to give away the end of the story, but suffice it to say that Nick's tale affirms the central premise of author Andy Crouch's *Culture Making*, the winner of *Christianity Today*'s 2009 Book Award for Christianity and Culture: The way to change culture is to create more of it. "So if we seek to change culture," Crouch writes, "we will have to create something new, something that will persuade our neighbors to set aside some existing set of cultural goods for our new proposal."[1]

This is not a new concept in the history of the Christian church, and particularly not for women in the church. "In just about every outbreak of a missional church movement in history, women have played a critical and up-front role," report missional church leaders Alan and Debra Hirsch.[2] Women were the backbone of the growth of Christianity in countries such as China and India; they were the main drivers in the explosive growth of the Korean church in the twentieth century. Women played a significant role in launching ministries, such as the Salvation Army, that concerned themselves with urban social justice needs. Women have had and will continue to make a significant impact on the world by creating culture in the manner that God has called them. Missional moms don't simply live counter to cultural pressures, but in ways small and large, they help shape the world for God's purposes. In addition to changing the world by creating missional families, some of today's inspiring moms are making an impact by creating tangible cultural products. Others are investing in "people-making" by serving and influencing the next generation. The examples that follow demonstrate just a small sampling of the many ways missional mothers are discovering their callings to shape and change culture.

The Missional Mom

MISSIONAL MOMS BRING
HEALING TO A WORLD OF SUFFERING

Missional moms are bringing healing in situations of desperation and huge need. Nadene Brunk is a certified nurse-midwife who traveled to Haiti for the first time in 2003 and who was appalled by the level of care available for pregnant and birthing mothers. What frustrated her most was that the women were sick with or dying from illnesses that were preventable. Nadene decided to do something about it.

In 2006 Nadene launched Midwives for Haiti, an organization that sends midwife volunteers to Haiti to train local Haitian nurses in midwifery and emergency obstetrics. A nurse trained in this way can see 120 pregnant women in a month for prenatal care and more safely deliver ten to twenty babies a month. Midwives for Haiti has already trained sixteen women and has begun hiring Haitian midwives to serve as teachers so the program can run even when American volunteers are not present.

At first Nadene found the needs overwhelming, and she had never led or launched an organization before. But after a great deal of soul-searching and prayer, she realized, "If I don't do this, no one will. This has been a new experience. I had no idea what I was getting into. But I would do it again, definitely. My life has been totally enriched by the Haitian people. I can't imagine my life without this project."

Remember my friend Jennifer Jao, the physician and a research fellow in infectious diseases at Mt. Sinai Hospital, who agonized over leaving her infant daughter while she went to Cameroon to conduct essential research? When she returned from her trip, she wrote a prayer letter about her experiences. Despite the pain of separation from her daughter, God certainly brought her to the right place at the right time:

My walk to my morning rounds at the Mbingo Baptist Hospital in Cameroon had been interrupted by Hosea, one of the midwives. "Dr.

Jao, do you have more of the breastmilk you've been pumping in the guesthouse? We need to give it to Blessing quickly." Blessing was a one-month old infant whose mother had just passed away from meningitis earlier that day. When I returned from the guesthouse with the milk, I saw Blessing's grandmother crying and her grandfather grieving with his head bowed down. Through a translator, the grandmother told me that Blessing had last eaten at 8 p.m. the previous night—twelve hours ago.

I looked at my frozen breastmilk and realized it would take another hour to thaw the milk, find a sterile bottle (hard to come by in Africa), and warm it. Blessing's cries became steadily weaker as she seemed to be losing hope of ever finding milk. My heart broke, and I did what only a lactating mother could do: I took the baby into my arms, opened my shirt, and let her nurse on me.

As I nursed Blessing, I caught a glimpse of God's redemption of this trip. She continued to nurse, and her crying ceased. We locked eyes, and I felt a wellspring of compassion inside me. "Perhaps this is a small taste of what Jesus feels for us," I thought. When I finally looked up, I saw a large circle of Cameroonians staring at me. Later, Eileen, my study coordinator explained, "We, as Africans, never imagined a white woman could ever serve a black baby in such a way."[3]

Despite the stress and strain of leaving her daughter for three weeks, Jennifer did more culture-making on that Cameroon trip than she likely ever imagined. She provided life-giving sustenance to another infant, which would not even have been possible had she not been a lactating mother. She demonstrated a profound expression of racial harmony that was a witness to the African women who watched her nursing Blessing. Someday this story will inspire her own daughter, even as it encourages those of us who also long to spread the fragrance of Christ in the world.

The Missional Mom

MISSIONAL MOMS ARE BRIDGE-BUILDERS
BETWEEN THE RESOURCED AND THE NEEDY

Moms come from a range of educational backgrounds and experiences, and missional moms in particular strive to use their schooling and vocational talents not for the purpose of fulfilling their own ambitions, but out of a sincere desire to live out God's calling in whatever locale or career He has placed them. Considering the numbers of women attending college, graduate, and professional school, even more possibilities will emerge in the future for moms to serve as culture-makers. Here are just two examples of the remarkable ways moms can serve as bridge-builders connecting those with many resources to those with few.

Mae Hong and Jennifer Jukanovich are two moms with a good deal in common. Both are parents of adopted children—Jennifer's family, you'll remember, includes two girls from China and a son from Rwanda; Mae's family includes two girls from South Korea and one biological daughter. Both women are well-educated, professionally gifted women with skills and experiences that would be any recruiter's dream. And both leverage those gifts and experiences to build bridges between "the least of these" and those who have the resources to help the needy.

Mae has more than fifteen years of experience in the field of philanthropy and currently directs the Chicago office of the Rockefeller Philanthropy Advisors. Her extensive experiences in philanthropy and social services administration have prepared her well for her current job, which is to advise ultra-high net worth individuals on how to be good stewards with their giving. "I believe that change is possible and problems can be fixed in our society," says Mae. "I have had the privilege of seeing firsthand how contributions of time, talent, and treasure have had direct impact on the lives of people and communities around them. And I help my clients find their own sense of how to change the world, to ask the right questions about stewardship and social responsibility, then help them to make decisions about their funds to solve the issues or problems they want to address."

Mae has been able to help donors support causes with tremendous culture-making impact. One of her donors "regularly gave contributions of $25,000 to $50,000 every year to a small community theater group that used powerful, compelling performance art to convey social justice messages and foster public dialogue." Another of Mae's donors "used her affluence and influence to create a nonprofit organization that fosters peace and reconciliation in conflict regions around the world, such as in Northern Ireland and Israel, through small-group dialogue."

Mae's role at RPA is all about finding the point of intersection where a person's resources meet the world's need, which sounds almost like a reiteration of that oft-quoted statement of Frederick Buechner's about calling being "where our deep gladness and the world's hunger meet." Mae sees her position uniquely influencing cultural change, and she takes her responsibility seriously. "My job puts me in a very rare and privileged role, and I feel placed there by God to, I hope, bring a perspective that benefits the kingdom either directly or indirectly," she says.

As for Jennifer, she and her family recently moved to Kigali, Rwanda, with two other families in order to launch Karisimbi Business Partners (www.karisimbipartners.com), an organization with the goal to "help alleviate poverty, build communities, and share the love of Christ by nurturing new and existing business enterprises" in Rwanda. Raising the funds and rallying the necessary support to make the move possible required all of Jennifer's God-given skills and then some, but it was clear God had prepared her for such a time as this. "I discovered that all the relationships and skills I'd built over fifteen years of working and serving in different capacities were leading up to this move," Jennifer says. "Now, I work for Karisimbi in the sense that I help with the fundraising portion, and I love to connect people I meet to the work we are doing. I am an advocate for those in need that I meet, and I love to connect people with resources, networks, and education to those who have a need or an idea."

Not long ago Jennifer discovered a two-year-old girl in her neighborhood who had been badly burned as an infant by a spilled oil lamp. "In this culture, she is considered deformed and she will have no future," Jennifer says. The same week she learned about this girl, her family had visitors from Boston. Both were doctors, and one happened to be a burn and trauma specialist. "I told him about this girl, just asking what he would recommend, and he said, 'Let's go and see her.' We went, and, he showed this child's mother how he was going to fix her daughter's hand—taking it from a crooked, deformed right arm to a straightened, beautiful arm."

Within a week, the doctor had connected with a plastic surgeon he knew was coming to Rwanda in the spring with Operation Smile and asked him to perform surgery on this girl's arm. Jennifer says, "Within a few months, this little girl went from having no future to being able to use her arm. Now she can go to school and learn to write. I literally stood in awe of how God places people in the right place at the right time—not for our own purposes, but to build His kingdom and love on others."

Through women like Jennifer and Mae, God is demonstrating that today's moms have significant opportunities to catalyze cultural change. Mae holds tangible influence in the direction of millions of dollars to bring significant solutions to very real societal problems. Jennifer's involvement in Karisimbi Business Partners is helping Rwandan entrepreneurs to build solutions that will change the future of a war-torn nation, and her presence in Rwanda has given her opportunities to connect people with needs to those with the resources to help. When you hear stories of people like Mae and Jennifer, you feel a sense of awe and amazement at what God can do through women who offer their talents and gifts to be used to change the world. And they are far from the only ones.

MISSIONAL MOMS LEVERAGE
THE POWER OF THE BLOG

Decades ago, if you were a woman with a message or with resources to offer others, you were restricted in how you could share that message with an audience. But times have changed, and today anyone can use the Internet to tell her stories or share her expertise with the global community. Blogging has become a powerful vehicle to allow people to express themselves, and missional moms have taken advantage of the freedom and flexibility of the medium to share about their personal challenges, offer wisdom, and make a difference in countless readers' lives.

Amy Julia Becker is one such mom. She has two children; her eldest, daughter Penny, has Down syndrome, which Amy Julia and her husband discovered two hours after she was born. As a way to help address the feelings and thoughts she experienced after the news about Penny, Amy Julia began blogging. At first it was a private blog, but then she noticed her friends were responding to her posts and passing them along to other people. "I realized my experiences could be an encouragement and a service to others, so I made a public version of the blog," Amy Julia says.

She was at her husband's fifteenth high school reunion when a woman Amy Julia did not even know told her she had read Amy Julia's blog about Penny. "She asked me, 'Can you tell me more about how your experience with God has shaped how you have worked through your situation with your daughter?' These kinds of moments have been a real confirmation that I am called to help people understand the intersection of the Christian faith with the realities and struggles of life."

God has opened up a much bigger audience for Amy Julia as further confirmation that He has called her to share her unique perspective and experiences. Recently Amy Julia signed a book deal to tell the story of her first two years with daughter Penny (*A Good and Perfect Gift*, Bethany House). Her blog now appears on the BeliefNet website (http://blog.beliefnet.com/thinplaces/), where she writes on topics related to faith, family, and disability. "I have an audience that is pretty diverse, which is encouraging," Amy Julia says. "I'm engaging a wide array of people on ideas and questions of faith, even as they know that I am a Christian. It's been the riskiest thing I've ever done, and yet it's also been the thing I've loved the most to do."

Remember Carisa Hinson, whose fears about the inner city changed so dramatically that God moved her and her family to the inner city of Philadelphia? In addition to her mission to reach out to local residents, this missional mom also ministers to home-schooling women through her blog http://1plus1plus1equals1. blogspot.com. Currently more than three thousand women follow the blog for Carisa's suggestions about how to teach their children; Carisa is a certified kindergarten teacher and uses her experience, her creativity, and her love for photography to create curriculum, offer suggestions, and minister to those she connects with online.

"I have received e-mails from women all over the world. I've had amazing opportunities to minister to people. I even had the chance personally to disciple a woman in Europe via e-mail," Carisa reports. "My blog has become a mission field for me."

Southern California mom Tonya Herman is another missional mom with a blog, which she created to show a different side of the city of Compton. Tired of the media representations of Compton that tended to focus on the stereotypical and negative aspects of the city, Tonya launched a website called "The Other Side of Comp-ton," with photos and photo essays depicting the hope and the gradual transformation of a city (www.theothersideofcompton. com). Tonya writes:

> People from both inside and outside the community are banding together in powerful ways to transform this city . . . Outside our com-munity, this journey toward transformation is still largely unrecog-nized. We, the people of Compton, believe that someday the changes lighting our city will spill out beyond our borders, and the world will

take notice. So I'm shining a light — I'm inviting anyone who will to see the *other* side of Compton, the side that I see . . . My God is a big God. Changing Compton is a huge task. Being in the midst of it *while* it's happening is an immeasurable honor. It is my family's privilege and our joy. Come walk with us for a moment, won't you? Come visit the other side of Compton.

If you take a moment to browse the photos, you will see a local high school being restored, community events with laughter and smiling children, youth development basketball programs in action, and clean city streets. Tonya's blog gives a life-filled and encouraging perspective of an under-resourced community and helps to debunk stereotypes that Compton is just about gangs and criminal activity. It is one missional mom's commitment to reflect light on the full picture of the city she loves. When visitors come to the site, they leave with a much different perspective on Compton and a desire to learn more about a city most people would be inclined to just ignore.

And the life and legacy of Mary Pearson, the cancer-stricken mother of my former babysitter, is also accessible through Caring Bridge.org (http://www.caringbridge.org/visit/ marypearson), which her family now maintains. Since Mary created the blog, it has had nearly 31,000 visits from family and friends. The design Mary chose for the blog prominently features the word "faith." I read every entry she posted, and I have never seen a note of despair, anger, or negative spirit. Just one month before she died, in the last post she was able to write, she was in the midst of grueling treatments and suffering from physical weakness. Yet she was still able to post, "The Lord is good all the time! Praying for you as I know many of you are suffering. Thank you for the prayers you raise up for my family and me," after which she quoted the famous verses from Philippians 4 with Paul's exhortation to "Rejoice in the Lord always." Even in her pain, to the end of her life on earth, Mary reflected a deep and inspiring sense of joy and gratitude.

Mary's words were the words of a woman who deeply loved and trusted in her Lord and a mother and wife who dearly loved her family. I have no doubt she has had visitors to her blog who have never even met her, like me, but who have been touched or even indelibly changed by reading her story. Such is the potential impact a single blog can have.

MISSIONAL MOMS ARE INVESTING IN THE NEXT GENERATION

Women have long been culture-makers through their investment in the next generation, either in formal or informal settings. While all moms are culture-makers in their homes as they train and raise their children, many of them additionally take on the responsibility of mentoring and teaching the next generation in intentional, purposeful ways. Here are the stories of several missional moms who are making culture to nurture the young.

I have never met or spoken with Marie Hazell. Yet her influence in my life, in my sons' lives, and in the lives of families all around the world, has been profound. Marie and her husband, David, are the founders of My Father's World (MFW), an organization that creates curricula for preschool through high school. One of the unique aspects of the MFW curriculum is how strongly it reflects a missional heart. Since 1998, more than 40,000 families have been influenced by My Father's World; these families are challenged to pray for missions and to think how they personally could become involved by praying, giving, and even going abroad. The Hazells started a nonprofit organization called "God's Word for the Nations" to provide money for Bible translation projects worldwide, which has raised more than a million and a half dollars in the past nine years.

This heart for missions stems from Marie's own experience as a missionary. Before becoming curriculum developers, the Hazells were missionaries in the field of Bible translation. Along with their six children, the Hazells lived in various parts of Russia, even spending time in the depths of Siberia where they assisted with printing the first Scripture portion in the Evenki language. After the Hazells moved back to the U.S., they launched My Father's World with a dual goal: to raise up generations of families who see the world through God's eyes and live according to that knowledge and to provide support for Bible translation. Marie Hazell has written all the MFW curricula herself, and the impact of her work has been far-reaching. This year, our family is using a curriculum written by Marie called "Exploring Countries and Cultures," which is an eye-opening experience for me and my kids as we journey into other worlds and lands, learn about missionary influences in those countries, and better comprehend the needs that exist all around the world. I am hoping for my sons' vision and understanding of the world to be expanded and their hearts to be softened toward global needs. If this happens, I will thank the Lord for Marie Hazell and her missional endeavors.

Culture-making can also occur as moms follow a calling to teach and mentor the younger generation. Christian women are teaching all over America, and sometimes in fields traditionally under-represented by women (and mothers). Mayling Wong-Squires is a mechanical engineer who has worked at the Fermi National Accelerator Laboratory in Batavia, Illinois (otherwise known as Fermilab) for the past thirteen years. Mayling is the mother of two children, five years old and younger. As a woman in a field largely dominated by men, Mayling feels a strong sense of calling to mentor other female engineers, and she has taken the initiative to meet with and encourage such women through-out her career. Currently Mayling helps oversee a Fermilab summer internship program for college students and mentors a female engineering student.

"Being an engineer is a huge part of my identity," Mayling says. "I want to share my experiences to help others who are trying to navigate their own career paths. I definitely believe God has called me to mentor other women in the field of engineering."

Mayling has been an example and a trailblazer at Fermilab, as one of the first female engineers to create a more flexible schedule that allows her to work part-time. "I've been hugely fortunate," Mayling says. "I have supervisors who tell me I'm doing good work, that I'm a good engineer, that I do the work of a full-time engineer. I feel God has been reassuring me that I'm doing okay, that my kids are okay. I count my blessings a lot. And now other women engineers at Fermilab are asking me about work-life balance, as they are about to become mothers themselves." Mayling's pursuit of God's calling has given her the culture-making opportunity to influence young lives and to change corporate policy as well, giving more women the future chance to live out their callings as engineer moms.

It's not easy to find many female physics professors or many Christian physics professors teaching the best and brightest young minds, but if you head to the campus of Swarthmore College in Pennsylvania, you will find the rare embodiment of both, as well as the mother of two children, ages thirteen and ten. Catherine Crouch is an associate professor of physics at Swarthmore and the wife of Andy Crouch, author of *Culture Making*. She has created a course for nonmajors planning a career in life sciences or medicine; she also enjoys teaching advanced courses for physics majors. As a teacher, she takes her mission seriously. "I see the core of my mission as introducing students to the beauty and orderliness of the natural world, and communicating my understanding that the world around us is a gift for us to take care of. Hopefully, with some of my students, I will have the opportunity to share where I believe this beauty and orderliness come from—the Creator— but I also hope that just studying with me helps my students see the world for what it really is," Catherine says.

Beyond communicating the intricacies of physics, Catherine hopes to present a credible witness that it is possible to be both intellectual about one's spiritual life and a Christian as well. She explains, "I hope that because I am part of the community at Swarthmore and known as a believer, students have evidence that being a serious follower of Jesus is not something you 'outgrow' in the process of becoming a scientist or scholar."

Catherine is a friend of mine from college, someone I have known since the very first days of school. She would never mention this in casual conversation, but she was the valedictorian of our graduating class and is easily one of the most brilliant people I know. Those of us who know Catherine personally can attest to the fact that her teaching position at an elite college makes absolute sense. Yet Catherine has struggled with questions of calling and purpose. "I feel like my combination of gifts, interests, and abilities match the real needs that exist in academia, and that being here is a genuine calling. But I also feel very strongly that I am called to invest time and energy in my children. Raising them is an equally important calling. The tough thing is that the academic career track doesn't make it easy to do both—though academia is easier than some careers," Catherine says.

As a working Christian mother with a strong sense of mission for what God is calling her to do vocationally, Catherine longs to see more people in the church wrestling with the question of how best to support Christian mothers in their quest for work-life balance. "I would like to see someone articulate a Christian vision for how the professions could make it more possible for parents, especially mothers, to divide their time more evenly between work and family. I don't see the church contributing as much as it could in that conversation. And I find I don't have many peers to talk with about how to navigate these kinds of situations."

Catherine brings up a crucial point: many, many mothers find the tension between workplace and home a barrier to pursuing the culture-making callings that God has placed before them. While it is beyond the scope of this book to delve into why the Christian subculture has not always or often been affirming of mothers in the workplace, I still want at least to encourage the church to find

The Missional Mom

ways to support mothers who feel strongly that God has gifted and called them into a career. Catherine and her husband, Andy, have been vigilant in careful parenting, particularly when their children were young, while still enabling Catherine to pursue her vocational calling. "It was wonderful how it worked out for me to work part-time for six years," Catherine says. "It was a difficult time professionally, in that I didn't make as much progress, but it was absolutely terrific for our family, so much better than working full-time, from when our son was born until he was six years old."

All the mothers I've introduced are working moms, working toward the various missions God has given them. I share Catherine's story to shine a light on one more amazing way God is using the gifts and passions of a missional woman to make a tangible impact in the lives of others. I have intentionally not often mentioned whether a mother I've highlighted in these pages is employed outside the home or not, because in truth the whole gamut of options is represented, and I feel it is too simplistic to label women as "stay-at-home" or "working." We know that *all* of us are working moms, working in whatever mix of family and other callings God puts before us. And all mothers need to be affirmed, supported, and encouraged to live out these God-given missions, whether they occur largely in the home or outside the home.

Do some women pursue professional gain for their own purposes? Of course, some do. Are some women staying at home ignoring a potential calling God is placing before them to be more missional in their lives? Again, I believe some are. But our missional focus is not about the question of whether a mother is employed or not outside the home. I wanted to answer my own question, "How are today's mothers living out the callings God has given them, in whatever context He has placed them?" The answers have come from women in a variety of life situations, which has convinced me all the more that we would do our mothers a better service to consider how to support them to live missionally, rather than defining their worth as mothers by whether or not they stay at home while raising their children.

The stories I could tell about today's culture-making moms are endless, and this small sampling in no way constitutes the full range of what missional moms are doing in the world to make a difference through culture-making activities, both within their homes and also through the particular missions God has given them. No doubt you know some inspiring missional mothers as well. As we find more ways to support those mothers in their efforts, women like Catherine and others won't feel so isolated from the rest of the church as they continue on their essential journeys as culture-makers in their respective fields.

If you have a story to tell about how God is using you to make cultural change, I'd like to invite you to help us celebrate moms as culture-makers. Visit *The Missional Mom* website (www. themissionalmom.com) and submit your own experiences so that we can encourage and support one another's efforts to be missional. (Or feel free to nominate other missional moms you are aware of!) This gets at the heart of what it means to be missional, which is a community activity, our focus in the next chapter.

CHAPTER TEN

The Missional Mom

The Missional Mom
Needs Missional
Community
(... and Vice Versa)

If you want to go fast, go alone.
If you want to go far, go together.
AFRICAN PROVERB[1]

When I was a graduate student at Wheaton College, I was part of the residence hall staff, and so I had to go to Honey-Rock Camp in the north woods of Wisconsin for a week of before-school bonding and team building with other staff members. I have to confess, I am not much of a camper. Once we arrived, my introverted self longed to be back in my climate-controlled apartment with indoor plumbing, and I felt out of place with the rest of my team. But then came the day we were to work through the ropes course together. A ropes course is a series of outdoor activities intended to be extremely challenging so that groups will

 develop teamwork and camaraderie. That sounded good in theory, until I saw The Wall. The Wall was simply a fifteen-foot tall wooden structure with a completely straight face and nothing protruding or available to hold on to. Our job was simple: using nothing but our own bodies, to get every member of our team up and over that wall, and to do it within fifteen minutes.[2]

On my own, there was absolutely no way I could have scaled that wall. None whatsoever. But that was, of course, the beauty of the assignment: it forced us to work in close partnership with our teammates to achieve the goal. When it was my turn to scale The Wall, I had teammates hoisting me up then pushing me from underneath, as well as people pulling me from above, while I did what I could by bracing my feet and scaling the face of the slippery wooden surface. When the last person had made it up and over, within the time limit, we were buoyed by what we had done. Banding together to work toward a seemingly impossible goal creates a sense of community that would not exist otherwise. I learned a critical lesson that day: when the task seems immeasurable, it's not just good but necessary to be in partnership with others.

The necessity for partnership is also true for missional moms, because living missionally can be an almost impossible task in our contemporary culture. It is much easier to be missional when you're in community with other mission-minded people. In this chapter, we'll look at the ways missional moms encourage and support one

The Missional Mom

another in their efforts to live in a countercultural way. We'll also find out from a number of today's missional church leaders what qualities distinguish these types of communities. We'll even address the question, "What do I do if I am *not* a part of a missional community?" The answer may very well surprise you.

MISSIONAL MOMS NEED
OTHER MISSIONAL MOMS

Scaling The Wall was only possible because my teammates and I were all moving the same direction; it would have been extremely difficult to achieve our goal if someone had been pulling us the other way. Similarly, missional moms find that having the support of like-minded missional moms is crucial in helping them move in a missional direction. Remember the three missional moms from Southern California? Rachel VerWys, Katy White, and Tonya Herman share longstanding friendships that help support them in missional living. Katy says, "I definitely favor, prefer, and feel much more at home with moms who are also missional. Friends who are really missional like Tonya and Rachel are essential for me, and I might burn out faster without them."

Rachel and Katy have been accountability partners who, for the past nine years, have continually asked themselves challenging questions to make sure their priorities are in line with what God would want for them. Rachel says, "I value our friendship deeply because of our similar passions and callings. Katy has encouraged me, supported me, and pushed me to become more holy and love Jesus and others well. Being missional is not a life one lives apart from community, and Katy is an integral part to sustaining a missional heart for me."

"In many ways, I think the number one driver of our friendship is the mutual desire to stay missional: to encourage each other to truly follow Jesus—as wives, as parents, as volunteers or workers in ministry, and as advocates for justice, mercy, and health in our world, communities, families, and selves," Katy adds.

Here in Chicagoland, I met with another pair of women whose friendship demonstrates how two missional moms can produce an "iron sharpening iron" effect in each other's lives. Betty Marmolejo and Josie Schopen attend Community Christian Church in Naperville and participate in Community 4:12, the church's compassion and justice ministry led by Kirsten Strand, whose story you read about in chapter 4. Josie is a stay-at-home mom with an eight-year-old daughter, and Betty, who has three kids, ages ten and older, is a part-time English Language Learner teacher at a local middle school. On the surface, Betty and Josie appear to be typical suburban moms. But in partnership, they have been a "brilliant team," according to Kirsten.

Last summer Josie and Betty began to work together to put a VBS program in place for the children in East Aurora, the low-income community adjacent to Naperville where CCC has a church site. Working in ministry together has catalyzed a friendship that helps both women feel supported and encouraged as they serve. "We took time not just to plan the event but to really get to know one another and build a relationship," says Betty. "That has really helped us when we are serving together, because I know she really gets me, and we complement one another's skills."

Betty and Josie say that being with other people committed to the mission of reaching out to the East Aurora residents has really solidified their own commitment. "Those who minister at Community 4:12 have become my family," Josie says. "And now the East Aurora ministry has become my ministry; it's where I'm supposed to be serving."

Betty adds, "What's great about being a part of Community 4:12 is that you see others stepping out in faith, and that is so appealing. Those are the kinds of people you want to be with and be like."

HOW MISSIONAL CHURCHES
ENCOURAGE MISSIONAL MOTHERHOOD

Betty, Josie, and Kirsten have found other missional moms as members of a missional church. How do these churches encourage moms to pursue missional lifestyles? Leading missional church practitioners report a number of common strategies for encouraging mothers to lead missional lives.

Missional churches affirm and celebrate missional moms when they find them. Missional churches that celebrate stories of ways mothers demonstrate a missional lifestyle spur other mothers to consider living in the same fashion. Julia Choi is one of the leaders of the Mom's Ministry at Newsong Church in Irvine, California. Choi says, "Whenever there is a mom who is passionate for a cause, we support her in every way we can so she can succeed." She shares story after story about the missional efforts among Newsong moms, such as the woman who raised more than $6,000 to build a well in Malawi by auctioning off art that the church's children created in Sunday school, or the mom who organizes monthly visits and weekly donations for a Mexican orphanage, or the group of mothers who felt burdened to help a boys' home in Tijuana. Whenever women at Newsong have the spark to engage in missional activity, their efforts are celebrated. "We as leaders are committed to equipping moms for a healthy spiritual life, and a missional purpose is built into that life," Choi says.

Bill White, outreach pastor of Emmanuel Reformed Church (ERC) in Paramount, California, says that, in addition to constantly talking about the mission of the church, he and his fellow pastors are always on the lookout for missional behavior, which they highlight from the pulpit for the encouragement of the entire congregation. "When I hear a story about a mom who decides to be missional and reach out to someone else, I will invite them both up to share their stories. We put a great deal of emphasis on telling stories of people in the church who have caught the vision of missional living," White says. (See Appendix A for an example of a joint testimony between two women at ERC, demonstrating one mom's obedience to God's call to take initiative in another mom's life.)

J. R. Briggs, pastor of a missional church called the Renew Community in Lansdale, Pennsylvania, agrees that churches need to let moms tell their stories. "A bunch of moms in a church in our area came together and wanted to do something about sex trafficking. They hosted a gigantic neighborhood yard sale—even the newspapers picked up on it—and they made $5,000 to battle sex trafficking in Southeast Asia. We need to encourage more activities like that, then tell those stories," Briggs says. "And the stories don't even need to be as dramatic as that. Just everyday stories about the ways moms are seeking to transform the lives of other people. Stories inspire more stories, so we commit ten minutes in each of our gatherings to do this."

Missional churches support the work women are doing, whether in or outside the home. As missional churches strive to share how moms are being missional, they also call attention to the wide breadth of what moms are doing in the world. Being missional is about using gifts and abilities to serve God and further His kingdom, and that can occur in a wide variety of contexts. Missional churches celebrate the various ways women do this, whether at home, or in the workplace, or in a ministry setting. "Moms, particularly with young children, experience a great deal of isolation, exhaustion, and guilt," says Briggs. "We need to acknowledge their efforts and let them know we hear those challenges. The church in North America does not do a good job of communicating that we understand and care about this difficult season and affirm the worthiness of mothering."

Similarly, mothers who work outside the home do not often find support for the ways they strive to live out their missional calling. "The mother in the workplace has so many different opportunities to minister there, as any workplace is an extension of the kingdom," says author and pastor David Fitch. "If God has placed you in a workplace, then every relationship is an opportunity to be used by God to be a witness to the gospel and to Jesus Christ. The church has to find ways to support and care for these moms as they are navigating the working world and also responsibilities at home." For example, pastors can make sure all the moms' ministry meetings are not scheduled during the daytime, when working moms are unable to participate. Or church leaders can ask mothers about their jobs and see what work-related prayer needs they might have.

Pastor Dave Ferguson of Community Christian Church believes that helping women see the bigger picture of who God has intended them to be is another way to encourage moms to become more missional. "Whether a woman is a stay-at-home mom or a working mom or somewhere in between, when she understands that she was made to be on a mission, her imagination begins to get sparked. Moms are some of the most creative people around. They are used to thinking up creative solutions to all kinds of life challenges."

Missional churches challenge cultural values that go against missional ones. Missional pastors do not shy away from addressing the cultural challenges parents face that make it difficult to lead missional lives. We've acknowledged the strength of cultural forces assailing our families such as materialism, consumerism, achievement orientation, and busyness. Churches that consistently tackle these issues head-on will encourage more missional ways of thinking. ERC's Bill White says, "I'm shameless about standing up in the pulpit and asking the congregation if they are invested in the spiritual development of their children. I like to ask, 'How many of you are praying that your children will become missionaries?' Erwin McManus says in *Unstoppable Forces* that he tells his son he's never going to pray for his safety, and we need to challenge our parents to do the same. We wage a constant battle against issues like desiring safety, comfort, and not succumbing to consumerism."

Briggs has noticed the busyness that has affected the families in his church. He says, "We need to be asking, 'What does it mean to have a healthy rhythm in our families?' There was a mother in our church who decided her kids were just going to participate in only one or two activities. The other moms were saying, 'I wish I could do that!' We need to affirm those who make countercultural choices. And we need to push against those tendencies to make idols of our family."

Missional churches encourage service along the lines of gifts, not roles. One of the challenges women experience in the church once they become mothers is that they begin to feel they are viewed primarily as mothers and not by the other gifts or callings that characterized them before they were moms. Caryn Rivadeneira, author of *Mama's Got a Fake I.D.*, writes, "Talk to three moms, and you'll find at least one (and more likely two or three) who have been hurt by the church's tendency to redefine women after they become moms . . . in our zeal to honor moms, we tend to dishonor women."[3] For example, once a woman becomes a mother, often she becomes another name to add to the list of volunteers for children's ministry duties. But not every woman is called to serve in children's ministry just because she herself has children.

"It is easy for us in the church to hit the default button for moms, that they should be serving in the children's ministry, but sometimes that is the last place they want to be especially if they have been with their kids all week," says Briggs. "We need to not make those assumptions and see where their interests and gifts are."

When church leaders take the initiative to understand the gifts and talents of the mothers in their congregations and encourage them to serve in those areas of giftedness, women are released to do so much more for the sake of the kingdom. At Community Christian Church, adults are encouraged to go through a "term group," essentially a temporary small group, in order to understand their personality type, their spiritual giftedness, and their passions. But members are not just encouraged to use that information to benefit the church. "We have many opportunities here at CCC for a mom to take a first step in serving, but we are certainly not limiting her to those opportunities. We love to hear how God might be leading each person to be on a mission wherever they are—home, work, school, or community," says pastor Dave Ferguson.

I remember a time when I was feeling the need to serve in multiple areas in our church—leading the children's worship, teaching a Sunday school class, being a part of the parents' council for the children's ministry, and being a small group leader. These were all worthy needs, but none at that point were truly my calling. I eventually burned out from doing too much and doing things not in line with my true ministry passions. In missional churches, the focus is on helping mothers express their giftedness rather than assuming what would be the best places for them to serve, then finding ways to affirm expressions of the giftedness whenever they occur in a response to God's calling.

Missional churches challenge husbands to be missional as well. Missional moms often cite the critical importance of missional husbands as a huge source of support. Each and every woman interviewed for this book mentioned the support of her spouse as vital to living out her missional calling. In many cases, these husbands have served alongside their wives in their wives' ministry efforts. What could be more affirming to a missional wife and mother than to have her husband's support to make her ministry dream a reality? Here are the comments of just a few of the women who lifted up their husbands as an influential part of their commitment to missional living.

Katy White, the inner-city physician who desires to launch her own health clinic one day, says, "Bill is a great support, because he reminds me often that this is what I'm called and created for. He prays for me, reminds me of my calling, tells me I do have leadership qualities when I'm doubting this, and allows me to do the things I need to, to encourage this sense of calling."

Remember the supportive husband who stayed home with his infant daughter while his wife made an essential trip to Africa?

Jennifer Jao says, "My life is doable given the man I've married. I don't think it would be doable if my spouse wasn't as supportive as he is."

"Without my husband, I couldn't do any of what I do. He has sacrificed far more than I have," reports Kirsten Strand, whose husband willingly supported their family's move to an under-resourced community. "You hear so often about things women do to support husbands in their careers, but it goes both ways."

My own husband took our three little boys to visit his parents for several weeks so that I could have the quiet and the time I needed to write this book. It was a wonderful, sacrificial expression of support. I am grateful beyond words, and I love the example my husband's support creates for our boys; he's modeling how important it is for a husband to support a wife's calling as well as the reverse. I'm reminded of those moving walkways in airport terminals, and how much farther and faster you travel when you use them. When missional moms have the encouragement of their husbands, they can go further and faster in pursuing their God-given missions. So churches that urge husbands both to be missional and to support their wives' callings perform a great service for their wives, for their families, and ultimately for the further-ance of God's kingdom.

Missional churches encourage moms both to "Bloom Where You're Planted" and "Go Where You'll Bloom." Mothers have so many opportunities to "bloom where they're planted," just by virtue of being mothers, and missional churches remind their moms frequently of the ways they can embrace their natural connections with other moms to help serve and love others. Pastor Larry Kim of Cambridge Community Fellowship Church of Cambridge, Massachusetts, which is located in an under-resourced part of the city, says, "At our church, it's become increasingly obvious that the way to reach our at-risk and single mothers is through other mothers. Once we identified the needs, it has felt natural and strategic to call forward the mothers in our congregation to serve.

I've realized that our mothers simply need to be connected with the people, the stories, and the ministry opportunities in our neighborhood."

But mothers can also be encouraged by church leaders to "go where they will bloom" as well as "blooming where they are planted." Sometimes, mothers need that gentle push from church leaders to step out of their comfort zones and try something a little different in order to live more missionally. Life on the Vine's David Fitch believes that "moms have so many wonderful opportunities open to them, they just have to take advantage of them. My wife chose to attend a local mom's group instead of a MOPS group or a church group, and she meets so many non-Christian women who all have immense needs and issues. There is a big empty black hole in our society on the question of how to raise children, and we can help point parents to the answers as we point them to their eternal purposes in Jesus. But first we have to go to where they're at."

Scot McKnight, professor at North Park University and author of the JesusCreed blog (www.patheos.com/community/Jesus Creed), which is widely read by missional leaders, offers a simple way of helping people understand what missional living is all about. "Being missional is about answering one simple question: 'How can I help you?' The missional response is to not to say, 'Give me a call if you need help.' It's about giving an active response. Women can ask this central question, whether they are in the workplace, at home, in a women's group. And pastors can encourage mothers to become intentional in this way."

A recent Baylor University study of Baptist families discovered that more than anything else, these families wanted their churches to help them to serve, even more than helping them with communication and marriage matters.[4] Missional pastors find ways to encourage not just moms, but their whole families to go and serve together. CCFC's Pastor Kim tells how his church experienced this desire from families to serve together. "Our church was recently challenged with this issue when we planned a missions trip to the Dominican Republic this summer. Two of the families were interested in going, but since we typically designed short-term missions trips for young singles and couples without children, we had to rethink how we would do the missions trip," Kim says. "We realized we need to be more thoughtful about being missional while including families. Even if parents become more missionally minded, what good is it if there are no opportunities for them to serve?"

Missional churches understand that when children serve with their parents, these children begin to embrace missional values at a young age. "We want tons of kids to serve in our Compton Initiative with their parents," says ERC's Bill White. "Our kids have been serving there from the beginning, and they have grown up loving to serve in Compton." As pastors and church leaders create opportunities for families, they might even lose some of those families who grow to love the neighborhoods they are serving so much that they actually relocate there, as happened with CCC's Kirsten Strand's family moving to East Aurora. But CCC's Pastor Ferguson could not be more pleased that Kirsten has done this and helped to birth a new church campus in East Aurora; this type of missional activity is exactly what he longs to see. In their book *Exponential*, brothers Dave and Jon Ferguson write, "We cannot build facilities big enough or fast enough to keep up with what God wants us to do. We need every follower of Christ engaged and mobilized in the movement."[5]

I was inspired, challenged, motivated, and energized by spending long periods of time with missional moms, their families, and their missional church leaders. Perhaps this is happening for you, too, as you read. Perhaps these missional ideas jive internally with what you may have been wondering and feeling for years—"Is this all there is to my Christian walk?"—and you desire to grow in the area of being more missional.

But some of you may be feeling disheartened and sobered as

you think about your own church community and networks. You may be asking yourself, "My church is so different from what I imagine a missional community should be. What are my options? What should I do?"

Here is my challenging answer to that question: *You* can be the one to start the missional revolution in your church.

YOU CAN START
A MISSIONAL REVOLUTION

At Community Christian Church in Naperville, the Ferguson brothers encourage members to leverage their existing interests and passions to discover their own mission fields. In fact, the first sentence in their book *Exponential* is, "A missional movement can start with you." CCC constantly reminds its members to dream about what particular mission God has given them to live out and pursue and then helps them to make those dreams a reality.

In your church, *you* can be the one to catalyze a missional perspective, to start your church's journey toward a lifestyle and vision for the church that involves looking outward and asking, as North Park's McKnight has suggested, "How can we help? How can our church focus less on what's going on inside our own walls and see how we can help the needs of the community and world around us?"

Although the concept of missional living seems like a trendy, recent hot topic among churches, ironically there is nothing new about the concept. If anything, the more accurate way to describe the missional movement is to say that it recaptures the legacy of the earliest Christians. So you would not be introducing radical ideas in your church family, as challenging as these ideas may sometimes appear. If you look back through the history of the church, you'll discover the growth of missional movements largely was driven by women. "Women have done the bulk of ministry in the West for a long, long time. Mothers are typically the most missional people in the church," McKnight says. "They hear the cries, they are the ones praying, they are in small groups, they are hearing about the needs. They are the ones helping people. We may not be regularly applying the word 'missional' to their activities, but that is in fact what they are doing."

With this rich legacy, women can certainly be the ones who catalyze a missional intensity in their congregations. What are ways you can encourage a missional perspective in your church?

- Read works by missional church leaders, and encourage your church leadership to read them, too. This chapter is available as a free download at www.themissionalmom.com/resources, as it's ideal for sharing with church leaders. There you will also find other recommended resources to help you and your church leaders become more missional.
- Start a small group book discussion about *The Missional Mom* and see how your group begins to answer the question, "How and where can we help further the mission of God both inside and outside the walls of our church? What are the needs among our church members, in our church neighborhood, or in our own neighborhoods, that we can address?" If you can localize these groups so moms who live in close proximity to one another study the book together, all the better. (Visit www.themissionalmom.com/resources for a free discussion guide to help you talk and share about the issues raised in the book.)
- In your groups, take an inventory of the gifts and passions represented. Brainstorm about how you can use those gifts and passions collectively to make a difference. Continually ask, "How is God calling us to help others in our friendships/playgroups/activities/workplaces/communities?"
- Encourage a culture of hospitality in the church as a way to practice more radical expressions later. Especially build opportunities for different groups to intersect—cross-life stage, cross-ethnic, cross-socioeconomic. Break down bar-

The Missional Mom

riers in the church and encourage fewer cliques and more connections. It is difficult to be missional as a church if there is not a culture of hospitality, especially toward those to whom we do not feel naturally drawn.

- Think about ways to let families serve together in the church. Encourage small groups or other ministry groups to do service projects together, including children if at all possible.
- Make serving and loving the poor and the under-resourced a priority in your church. Devote financial and people resources to this ministry and encourage your leaders to highlight the resulting stories from the pulpit.
- Create accountability groups of no more than two or three people in which you are regularly asking each other challenging questions, particularly with regard to standing firm against cultural forces that work against being missional. (See Appendix B for examples and ideas.)
- If your small group reads *The Missional Mom* and starts catching the vision to be more missional, have as many people from the group lead other groups to pass along the same ideas. Always think about multiplying your efforts going forward.

Anyone can be missional; everyone can be missional; everyone is called to be missional. The more people who are talking about missional ideas at your church, the faster the ideas can spread. Take the initiative and the risk to start making it happen. But whatever you do, don't try to be missional all on your own. That's a hard wall to climb all by yourself.

The calling God gives us all is the same, whether we live in a community with visible needs or in a well-resourced community where everything appears on the surface to be perfect—or somewhere in between. God's calling is for all Christ-followers: Go and love and serve others. Go and make disciples. Go and be missional.

Whatever you do, *go* out into the world and make a difference. If you are willing, God can do amazing things in and through you.

The Peace Corp has a motto: "Life is calling. How far will you go?" For our purposes, let's modify the saying just a bit: God is calling. How far will you go? Being a missional mom is all about saying, "I am willing. I will go where you want me to go." The Wall awaits. It may seem insurmountable, but go grab a team, and start climbing! You will be amazed at what God can do through you as you start working together.

CHAPTER 11

The Missional Mom
Surrenders All

I surrender all, I surrender all,
all to thee, my blessed Savior,
I surrender all.

JUDSON W. VAN DEVENTER

It would hardly be fair for me to encourage moms everywhere to be missional without sharing how God has been changing my own life as I've attempted to keep His calling at the center of all my decisions.

Most recently God took my desires to live missionally and surprised me by leading me to focus on my children's education as our family began homeschooling. Homeschooling became, for me, one of the ways I put missional ideas into real life.

In the spring of 2009 I was meeting with Sue Ferguson, the wife of Community Christian Church's lead pastor, Dave Ferguson, and currently the director of term groups at the church. Sue's husband calls his wife "the most missional mom I know." I had no idea that meeting Sue would lead to some big changes for our own family.

Sue said to me, in the process of telling me her own story, "I've learned as a parent, never say never. I never thought I'd homeschool. We had our kids in private school, but it became unaffordable. God sent people into my life who introduced me to new ideas, so then we thought, *maybe* we'll homeschool. We were really praying about it. Then we went to this conference, and God led us to understand why homeschooling would be beneficial for us. I was in between laughing and crying, saying to Dave, 'I think we're supposed to homeschool!' My mother-in-law wisely reminded me, 'You can always change your mind.' So we took the jump, and we never looked back."

For reasons only God knows in full, Sue's comments about homeschooling stuck with me. I had never considered homeschooling before that moment. I am a product of the public schools, and we were living in a city known for its excellent public schools. Homeschooling made no sense. Yet I still felt that gentle nudging from God: "I want you to look into this."

With great reluctance, I did what Sue did: I started to research. I started to check out websites and became more knowledgeable about what homeschooling entailed, what the legal requirements were in Illinois, what kinds of curricula were out there for children of my sons' ages, and what the pros and cons were. I only personally knew two families who had homeschooled, and both lived far away. I spoke with each one and learned more about their experiences. I met a friend of a friend who graciously gave me an evening to hash out all my questions. And I prayed. And then I prayed some more.

Along the way I clued in my husband about this journey I was on. He was supportive and open to wherever God was leading us, but he knew the responsibilities would largely fall on my shoulders and the decision would ultimately have to be mine. His encouragement and openness were huge blessings and allowed me to continue on this road of discovery. In the end, to make a long story short, we sent in our letter to the local school, informing them that our eldest son would not be attending second grade there but would be homeschooled instead. We are now in our second year of homeschooling, with a third grader, a kinder-gartener, and a preschooler in our "class." And, despite all my doubts and fears before we took this leap of faith, my family would all unequivocally say the experience has been extremely positive so far. And as for me? I've been completely surprised by how much I've loved it.

Obviously, God is not calling all missional moms to home-school their children. Many women find their connections through the local public schools a powerful bridge for ministry. The point is not to push homeschooling as the ultimate education option but to use my experience as an example of how you might welcome a fresh idea or spiritual nudge from the Lord.

The feeling I had after speaking with Sue was an unmistakable nudging from the Lord, and maybe you have felt a similar nudge to look more closely at a particular aspect of your life. Start small. Ask the Lord for direction on what *one thing* you might focus on for you potentially to change or to work on. For example, maybe you've experienced a conviction about reducing the busyness or the consumerism in your family's life. Maybe you are feeling a longing to do more to reach "the least of these" somehow. Perhaps you want to embrace a Third-Culture perspective and reach out to someone from a different racial or ethnic background. Maybe you wonder how a certain gift and talent might be used more intentionally to serve the Lord. Whatever that one thing is, take some time to focus on that area and see where the Lord leads you.

Pray, research if you need to, and pray some more. Talk with someone about what you are feeling and the journey you are on so that you don't travel it alone. Let your spouse know, and find another friend or two who will be supportive and walk alongside you as you become a more missional mom. As you stay open to where God is leading your heart, mind, and soul, be ready for God to present you with initial steps toward changing that one thing in your life.

Then take that first step, which also means taking a leap of faith of some kind. For that reason, the first step is often the hardest step. But once you make that leap, you may discover it wasn't as hard as you expected. You might in fact discover that what God is calling you to, however scary or uncomfortable it might seem, becomes a huge blessing and an affirmation that you are doing God's will.

For me, my uncertainties about homeschooling centered on the ramifications of taking my kids out of the public schools. Would it be best for them educationally? But then I sensed the Lord challenging me on what I meant by "best." Was I using the world's standards, and was I being overly influenced by an achievement-oriented culture to define success? I came to realize that, for me, homeschooling was a way to repudiate my former dependence on the success narrative that had shaped me and that I was consequently using to shape our kids.

Another leap of faith for me was also to trust that God was in control of our children's future, that I did not need to worry about what their SAT scores would be or what college they would go to someday, and that His best for them was different from what the world said was best for them. For us, choosing to homeschool has been a missional decision, as it has helped us break free from some of the snares that had entrapped us with regard to wanting our kids to "succeed." Of course, I hope we are giving our kids a quality education here at home, and our standards for what we would like them to learn remain high. But I no longer think of quality as being judged by whether my kids score well on standardized tests or get into the gifted class. Homeschooling has also freed us

The Missional Mom

to think more about where we want to live long-term; assuming we continue to teach our kids at home, we are no longer bound by considering locations with strong school districts. We can potentially live anywhere God calls us, which is exciting and freeing on so many levels.

Sue encouraged me never to say, "Never." It remains to be seen how long God will lead us down this new path. But regardless of how long our homeschooling journey lasts, it has already given me a sense of adventure and excitement about being a mom that had previously been missing. It has given me a sense of purpose for how I can use my gifts as someone who loves to learn and pass knowledge on to others, as I train my children so they will one day similarly use their gifts and callings for the Lord's purposes.

Whatever adventure God has in store for you, for your growth and His glory, my prayer for you has been and continues to be that you will hear that small, still voice, and that you will be open to how God might want to change you, and change your life, in a more missional way. Be prepared: Living the missional life can be exhausting! This past year has probably been the hardest in my life—trying to work on this book, teaching my kids, serving at church when possible, and of course cooking, cleaning, doing the laundry and grocery shopping! But this past year has also been my most fulfilling, exciting, and enjoyable year. There is something about taking a risk and then pursuing a calling God has given you that is ultimately so freeing. In the introduction to this book, I asked whether being a missional mom can help women experience more joy, peace, and fulfillment in their motherhood journeys. Having met and spoken with the missional moms you've read about, as well as following God's call on me in the area of homeschooling, I can unequivocally report that the answer to the question is absolutely "Yes."

I probably don't always look and act like the triumphant, excited, unburdened mom pictured on the cover of this book. I have my challenging days and my tear-my-hair-out days and my days when I wonder if I'm doing the right things. But the Lord finds ways to fill me with affirmation and encouragement when I am living out the mission He has given me—when I've worked on my writing or when I've been immersed in planning for school, for example. And that deep sense of peace, fulfillment, and excitement characterizes the motherhood experience God has in mind for us all. I firmly believe that one way we can achieve that kind of motherhood is by pursuing a more missional lifestyle.

What is the mission God has in mind for you? Just keep asking this question of yourself and of God. If you sincerely are open to the answer, He will reveal it to you. Then be ready to respond and step forward in faith to accept the mission, wherever it takes you.

WORDS OF ADVICE ON YOUR JOURNEY

To help you on your journey toward embracing a more missional lifestyle, here is some of the wisdom I have gleaned from the inspiring missional moms I know.

Offer grace, not judgment, to other moms. My wise friend Caryn Rivadeneira writes, "We moms are not always the most supportive of one another. How many times have you looked at another mom's parenting style, career choices, or personal lifestyle and decided to take her to task in your mind?"[1] If this book in any way results in making you feel guilty about your choices or judgmental toward others for theirs, then we have all missed the mark. The stories of the women you've met through this book are meant to inspire and encourage you to ask the Lord how you might live more purposefully for Him, with the understanding and recognition that we are all God-created unique works in progress. Comparing our situation with other women will only lead to heartache and frustration. Heidi Bratton, author of *Making Peace With Motherhood*, writes, "Many of the expectations of what mothering will be like that we assume from our peers are misleading at best. We've, none of us, been down this parenting road before. We do not have the same spouses, incomes, in-laws, education, number of personalities of children, housing options, or schooling options. . . . We should not expect to mother in the same way as our peers mother."[2] If you experience resistance or backlash as you talk about missional ideas, please do not let Satan use your differences as a way to bring division to the body. "Let your conversation be always full of grace," Paul writes in his letter to the Colossians, and "seasoned with salt" (Colossians 4:6). In other words, feel free to bring up topics that could be controversial, such as being countercultural, but do so with attitudes of grace and not condemnation.

This same principle applies to how you view yourself and your children. Yes, we mothers have a great amount of influence in our children's lives. But sometimes I think we err too much on the side of believing we have *so* much influence on our kids that when they stray or go in a direction we don't like, we are entirely to blame. But "we must be clear about our own limits. We are not capable of producing perfect followers of Christ, as if we were perfect ourselves. Our work cannot purchase anyone else's salvation or sanctification. . . . We will parent imperfectly, our children will make their own choices, and God will mysteriously and wondrously use it all to advance his kingdom," writes Leslie Leyland Fields.[3] Give yourself, your friends, your family, and your children a great deal of grace as you journey together toward a deeper understanding of the missional life.

Recognize there are seasons and limits to your life. Our generation of mothers is learning that we cannot do it all, as much as we wish we could. Another wise friend of mine, Grace Shim, is a missionary with the Evangelical Covenant Church in Thailand. We were once talking about how to balance all the callings we have, and she told me something I have never forgotten, that balance is not something necessarily to achieve in a 24-hour period, but over the course of one's life. There will be seasons when our children necessarily require a great deal of our energy and attention, especially when they are young. We can still find ways to be missional in those seasons while recognizing and embracing our limitations—we can stay in prayer about causes we care about or about church activities or programs we might not be able to participate in. We can find an hour of time, perhaps, during the week to make some calls or stuff some envelopes or make a meal for someone in need. If our children are old enough, we can bring them with us and serve as a family. We can all create opportunities to be missional, no matter what our circumstances.

When your children are very young, you will necessarily have to focus more on their needs, and you can embrace that season while recognizing that it is just a season, which will soon pass. "After I started to have my kids, my world got really small," says Shayne Moore, the "Global Soccer Mom." "I wish someone would have told me that was appropriate, that it was okay my world became smaller when I started to have babies."

Elisa Morgan, president emeritus of MOPS International and publisher of *Fullfill* (www.FullFill.org), an online resource encouraging leadership development in women of all stages and spheres, says that "women need to give themselves a great deal of grace. Most of the time, we are not going to have our most effective influencing years outwardly when our children are very young. There is a 'me' inside 'mommy' that needs to be stewarded, and we're as responsible for that as we are for raising our children."

As you seek to be missional, you may come across limits of time, energy, and resources, especially because your life as a mother necessarily entails caring for others in addition to yourself. Accept those limits, with the knowledge that your most fruitful years of ministry may come later. Katy White's dream is to open a health clinic in Compton, California, but she knows she does not have the capacity to do it now, with two elementary-school-aged children. "I can't be a mom and start a clinic right now," Katy says. "It's a full-time job to start a clinic, but I'd be neglecting my kids to do so. But I'm thankful I've been able to find clinics to work at part-time, which will help me when the time comes for me to launch one someday."

Mae Hong, the high-level philanthropy advisor, became the parent of three girls within the span of seven months. Mae and her husband, Bob, adopted two young sisters from South Korea, and within the same year, their third daughter was born. Mae had to learn quickly that what she had been doing before she had children would necessarily change. "That was my first lesson in motherhood— you can't do it all," Mae says. "It's hard sometimes for women to accept this as reality. But doing so in my own life has been really helpful in being a mother. I'm very comfortable now living within my limitations."

I'm reminded again of the story from the life of Jesus about the little boy who shared his five loaves of bread and three fish. Jesus used what seemed like a small offering to bless the masses abundantly. Whatever we offer to the Lord with a willing and faithful heart, He can use in ways we cannot even imagine or expect. Our offerings may feel insufficient. I know I cannot write a book that makes every point I wanted to make and tells every story I wanted to share. I know my year of teaching my boys will have its difficult days and unmet goals. I have to accept my limitations of time and energy. I can only do so much. I am trusting God to use my expressions of culture-making, flawed and finite though they are, to make a difference in people's lives as He sees fit. The amazing thing about accepting our limitations is that it opens our eyes to the wondrous ways God can do immeasurably more than we could ever ask or imagine.

Remember our first and foremost calling. Nothing we seek to "do" for God is as important as our actual relationship *with* God. Keith Meyer is a "Missional Coach of Pastors" and teaches at Denver Seminary on leading and developing missional communities of transformation. He says, "The only way to actually get missional in your life is to begin to enter into a life of intentional formation with Jesus. Until people really have Jesus as their teacher, participating in life with Him on a moment by moment basis, then all the talk about being missional doesn't go anywhere."[4]

Missiologist Ed Stetzer and coauthor Philip Nation express a similar idea in their book *Compelled by Love: The Most Excellent Way to Missional Living.* "Missional ministry can only be accomplished provided there is a sure foundation for all we do. We begin with the knowledge of God because the mission originates in His heart. Otherwise, we will find ourselves doing many of the good things possible in this world, but never accomplishing the one great thing for the kingdom God had in store for us."[5]

Don't let anything, even the teaching of this book, take you away from that one *great* thing God has in store for you, which is a deeper understanding and knowledge of who He is that comes from being *with* Him in all that you do. Being missional will flow from your relationship with Him.

FINAL HOPES AND DREAMS . . .

My hope and prayer for you is the one the apostle Paul expressed to the Philippian church: "That your love may abound more and more in knowledge and depth of insight, so that you may be able to discern what is best and may be pure and blameless until the day of Christ, filled with the fruit of righteousness that comes through Jesus Christ—to the glory and praise of God" (Philippians 1:9–11). If you have found this book helpful in your own faith journey, I would be so encouraged to hear about it. Visit the book's website at www.themissionalmom.com and share what you've learned with me and with others. I hope the site will become a virtual community for helping to spur one another on to missional living, for God's glory and purposes. In closing, let me offer you the following Franciscan benediction:

May God bless you with discomfort
At easy answers, half-truths and superficial relationships

So that you may live deep within your heart

May God bless you with anger
At injustice, oppression and exploitation of people
So that you may work for justice, freedom and peace

May God bless you with tears
To shed for those who suffer pain, rejection, hunger and war
So that you may reach out your hand to comfort them and
To turn their pain into joy

May God bless you with foolishness
To believe that you can make a difference in the world
So that you can do what others claim cannot be done
To bring justice and kindness to all our children and the poor[6]

"Missional" might be a newer word in the Christian vernacular, but the call for Christians has remained the same since the beginning: to remain in Jesus and surrender all to Him as He has surrendered Himself for us. Go forth, with God, and bring his light, love, peace, and joy to a world that desperately needs it. And never forget that you can make a difference as you allow the immeasurable power of God to work through you. A broken world awaits, and all God asks for is your willingness to follow Him. *God is calling. How far will you go?* My hope and prayer for you, as it is for myself, is that we would be able to answer, "I surrender all, Lord. I will go as far as it takes." In the end, God's call is the only mission worth our wholehearted passion and devotion.

APPENDIX A

A Tale of Two Moms

Cheryl Chamberlain and Karla Kroese Testimony
EMMANUEL REFORMED CHURCH, PARAMOUNT, CA
Sunday, October 22, 2006

Cheryl

I was not raised in the church. From a young age my mom did teach about some spiritual things, so there was a seed planted. It just took quite a few years for that seed to be watered and my faith to begin growing.

In the fall of 2003, Jason and I started contemplating going to church, but we didn't act on it. Our neighbor Alicia Streelman even gave us an invitation to Christmas Eve that year, but it wasn't our time yet. It was around this time I started running into Karla Kroese all the time—at the play area at the mall, at the polling station, and at Target. After seeing her around so much but never meeting, I started to wonder who she was.

Karla

About two and a half years ago, I wasn't looking to have any more friends. I had plenty of friends, plus I had four kids under the age of four! But I kept running into this girl all over the place, and I was confused as to why it was happening so much. My husband recommended that I pray about it. I didn't want to do that, though, because then I knew I'd actually have to take action and make something happen. So I continued having inner battles over why this girl kept entering my life, and what exactly I was supposed to do about it. The time I saw her at the polling station and exchanged hellos, I realized God was calling me to take action. I just didn't think I had the energy to invest in another relationship. So I prayed and I made the decision to be obedient and introduce myself the next time I saw her.

About a week later I was in line at customer service at Target, and there she was checking out at the register. I honestly thought that if I didn't look at her, maybe I wouldn't have to say anything. But, we made eye contact and exchanged friendly hellos as usual, all the while this big booming voice in my head saying, "TAKE ACTION." I let out a big sigh, corralled my kids, left the line, and ran after her. We introduced ourselves and made a connection immediately. At this point I didn't know what to do next, so I began praying about it and wrestling with what to do.

On the afternoon of Easter Sunday, 2004, my thoughts were so preoccupied with this girl that I met I couldn't even focus. God just wouldn't let it rest. I thought and I prayed, and I finally asked Bill if he wouldn't mind taking a walk past her house with the kids since they lived in our neighborhood.

As we were approaching their house I could see they weren't home—I felt disappointed, but, hey, I tried. Just as we reached

The Missional Mom

their driveway, though, the Chamberlains came walking from the house across the street.

Cheryl

In the first few months of 2004, I grew more serious about the idea of finding a church. Then, finally, on Easter Sunday 2004 we visited our first church. It was in Bellflower. It was an okay experience, but nothing I was interested in repeating. It would be weeks before we tried another one, and I don't even know why we went back. Except that God was starting to pull on us.

But the best thing about Easter Sunday 2004 was that we had an amazing "coincidence" happen that afternoon. Right when we were returning home from visiting with some family, we saw Karla and her whole family walking down our street. I couldn't believe it. We had a great time talking with Karla and Bill, and our kids had fun together. We swapped phone numbers, and even set up a play date that week.

Karla

Early on, it was evident that she was not a believer. But I enjoyed Cheryl, and for months we kept having play dates and talking on the phone. I kept praying for an opportunity to introduce her to Jesus Christ, or in the least, to Emmanuel. I also kept introducing her to friends from church, and to be honest, I kind of hoped that they might do the scary work of inviting her for me. But I was the one who really had the relationship with Cheryl. And one day that conversation came. And a whole lot more.

Cheryl

In a conversation one day I shared with Karla that Jason and I were trying to make a go of it at a church. Karla extended an invitation to Emmanuel and asked that we "just try it" before we put roots down anywhere. We came that Sunday and never looked back. It was the small things that made the difference—having someone to talk to in the courtyard after church, having Karla and Bill's friends welcome us in, and getting a personal invitation to Alpha [a ten-week course allowing people to explore questions about God and the Christian faith].

I had many days when I just wanted to give up because trying to figure this faith out was just too hard. Strangely enough, this person that had been placed in my life—this new friend—was the only person in the world that I could openly share all of these feelings with and not fear criticism or judgment. Karla offered her shoulder to me countless times. She always made herself available, and she gave me the strength to continue walking down that scary road. Karla prayed me through Alpha, where I was finally able to surrender the control of my life to Christ. I don't believe that I could have done it without her!

Karla

I also had the privilege of having coffee with Cheryl the day that she and Jason prayed together and Jason gave his life to Christ. And I got to stand up with her and her family right here on the day she and Jason and the kids were baptized and became Partners in Mission. And I got to see how the blessing comes back around. Besides enjoying her friendship, my kids enjoy their kids. And it was Cheryl's son Nikolas who one day asked my son Seth if his name was written in the Book of Life. That conversation led to me praying with my boy to accept Christ in his heart.

Two and a half years ago I didn't need any more friends. Or so I thought. What was really going on is that I was complacent in my faith, and God was calling me to invest. I'm so glad I did. Thank you.

The Missional Mom

APPENDIX B

Accountability
Questions

Accountability Questions for Adults

1. Where did you see God working this week?
2. What Scripture has most affected you this week? Why?
3. Have you given in to vanity or flirtatiousness this week?
4. Have you been tempted by or exposed to sexually alluring material, or entertained inappropriate sexual thoughts this week?
5. Have you lived in integrity and generosity in personal, family, and/or business finances?
6. How have your words built up or torn down others or self? Have you exposed yourself or contributed to gossip?
7. Have you done your 100 percent best in your job, school, family, etc.?
8. How have you invested (or failed to invest) in your family and friends this week?

9. How have you been investing in relationships with unchurched people this week?

10. Do you feel you missed any opportunities to talk to people about the Lord?

11. Have you taken care of your body through exercise and good eating/sleeping habits?

12. Which fruit of the Spirit have you had the hardest time living? Why?

13. What pressures have you faced this week to conform to the world's standards and not God's?

14. When this week have you had an opportunity to do an act of kindness toward someone? What did you do?

15. Have you lied or left anything hidden in answering these questions?

Accountability Questions for Parents

1. Did you hug your children today and tell them you loved them?

2. Did you pray and share Scripture with your children daily?

3. How did you make your children feel special this week?

4. How have you seen God working in your children this week?

5. Did you demonstrate inappropriate criticism, nagging, or anger toward your family this week?

6. Did you ask your children for forgiveness when you sinned against them?

Accountability Questions for Couples

1. Have we prayed together this week? Shared Scripture together?

2. What were our best moments this week? Our worst moments?

3. How can I pray for you this week?

4. Is there anything we need to forgive each other for?

The Missional Mom

5. Have we spent our time wisely around the home this week?
6. When is our next date night?

Accountability Questions for Small Children

1. What are you thankful for today?
2. What are you sorry for today?
3. What are you hopeful about for tomorrow?

Notes

Introduction: What Happened to the Joy of Parenting?

1. Although there may no longer be more live feeds of Molly the Barn Owl, you can see more information about her at http://mollysbox.wordpress.com/.

2. Caryn Rivadeneira, *Mama's Got a Fake I.D.* (Colorado Springs: WaterBrook Press, 2009), 3.

3. Blog post, "Why Parents Hate Parenting," www.themommyrevolution. wordpress.com, July 10, 2010, see comments.

4. Some notable exceptions: *The Myth of the Perfect Mother* by Carla Barnhill, *Mama's Got a Fake I.D.* by Caryn Rivadeneira, and *Parenting Is Your Highest Calling* by Leslie Leyland Fields.

5. Certainly another source of tension for many of today's mothers who work outside the home is the lack of support these women generally experience from their workplaces to achieve greater work-life balance, not to mention from non-family-friendly policies in this country. In Neil Gilbert's book *A Mother's Work: How Feminism, the Market, and Policy Shape Family Life*, he writes, "Compared to the industrial democracies of Europe, the United States is considered a laggard in dispensing parental leave, day care, and other publicly subsidized emollients to diminish the friction between raising a family and holding a job" (p. 125). It is beyond the scope of this book to tackle the larger societal issues resulting in the United States being one of the more difficult countries to be a mother, but I wanted to acknowledge the reality that for mothers working outside the home, trying to juggle the

desire to be a devoted mother along with the call to a particular vocation is challenging in the U.S. especially.

6. Darrell Guder, ed. *Missional Church: A Vision for the Sending of the Church in North America* (Grand Rapids, MI: Eerdmans, 1998).

7. Alan Hirsch's book is considered "faithful to the original definition outlined by Guder," *Leadership Journal*, Fall 2008, 21.

8. Rivadeneira, 33.

Chapter 1: The Missional Mom Embraces the Call of Her Missional God

1. http://www.ushmm.org/education/foreducators/resource/pdf/resistance.pdf.

2. Os Guinness, *The Call* (Nashville: Word, 1998), 8.

3. Skye Jethani, sermon at Mars Hill Bible Church, June 20, 2010. You can find the sermon in its entirety at www.skyejethani.com/message-from-mars-hill-with/575/. I am deeply grateful for Skye's words in this sermon and highly recommend listening to it.

4. Guinness, 31.

5. Rodney Clapp, *Families at the Crossroads* (Downers Grove, IL: InterVarsity Press, 1993), 156.

Chapter 2: The Missional Mom Resists Cultural Pressures

1. FromAlan Hirsch, *The Forgotten Ways: Reactivating the Missional Church* (Grand Rapids, MI: Brazos, 2006), 111. Thanks to Bill White for alerting me to this quote.

2. Reference to Andy Crouch's excellent work *Culture Making: Recovering our Creative Calling* (Downers Grove, IL: InterVarsity Press), 2009.

3. A reference to this quote: "What contemporary American culture advertises is achievement and accomplishment as the route to ultimate happiness," says Suniya Luthar, a professor of psychology and education at Columbia University in New York; appears in "Gen Nexters Have Their Hands Full," Sharon Jayson, *USA Today*, August 20, 2006. www.usatoday.com/news/nation/2006-08-20-generation-next_x.htm.

4. "America's Best High Schools," *Newsweek*, June 13, 2010. This year WWHS was in the top 100, at #85. www.newsweek.com/feature/2010/americas-best-high-schools/list.html.

5. Alexandra Robbins, *The Overachievers: The Secret Lives of Driven Kids* (New York: Hyperion, 2006), 17.

6. Leslie Leyland Fields, *Parenting Is Your Highest Calling: And Eight Other Myths That Trap Us In Worry and Guilt* (Colorado Springs: WaterBrook Press, 2008), 174.

7. Robbins, 216.

The Missional Mom

8. Nancy Gibbs, "The Case Against Over-Parenting," *Time*, November 20, 2009.

9. Ed Young, *Kid CEO* (Nashville: Faith Words, 2004), 16.

10. The specific findings were as follows: • Parents are receiving carefully marketed messages that good parents expose their children to every opportunity to excel, buy a plethora of enrichment tools, and ensure their children participate in a wide variety of activities.• Highly scheduled children have less time for free, child-driven, creative play, which offers benefits that may be protective against the effects of pressure and stress. • Childhood and adolescent depression is on the rise through the college years. •Many parents seem to feel as though they are running on a treadmill to keep up yet dare not slow their pace for fear their children will fall behind. You can find the report at http://www.aap.org/pressroom/playfinal.pdf.

11. Scottie May, associate professor of Christian formation and ministry, Wheaton College, personal interview, March 12, 2010.

12. Tracey Bianchi, *Green Mama: The Guilt-Free Guide to Helping You and Your Kids Save the Planet* (Grand Rapids, MI: Zondervan, 2010), 67.

13. Soong-Chan Rah, *The Next Evangelicalism* (Downers Grove, IL: InterVarsity Press, 2009), 48. The context of this reference is that Rah notes that post-9/11, president George W. Bush encouraged Americans to shop in order to keep the American economy strong.

14. Mary Ellen Ashcroft, *Balancing Act: How Women Can Lose Their Roles and Find Their Callings* (Downers Grove, IL: InterVarsity Press, 1996).

15. Fields, 67.

16. For an excellent discussion of how American Christianity has been influenced by cultural forces, see what Soong-Chan Rah, associate professor of church growth and evangelism at North Park Theological Seminary in Chicago, has to say about the tie between Christian and American culture in his book *The Next Evangelicalism*: "The church remains the church, but we more accurately reflect the culture around us rather than the characteristics of the bride of Christ. We are held captive to the culture that surrounds us. . . . American Christianity has acquiesced to the materialistic values of American society and is no longer distinguishable in its values and norms from the excessive materialism of American society."

17. May interview, March 12, 2010.

Chapter 3: The Missional Mom Is a Culture Rebel

1. http://en.wikipedia.org/wiki/File:Williams_College_-_Haystack_Monument.JPG (public domain photo).

2. Dave Ferguson, Jon Ferguson, Eric Bramlett, *The Big Idea* (Grand Rapids, MI: Zondervan, 2007), 16.

3. Shane Claiborne, *Irresistible Revolution* (Grand Rapids, MI: Zondervan, 2006), 136.

4. Os Guinness, *The Call* (Nashville: Word Publishing, 1998), 221.

5. Dave Goetz, *Death by Suburb* (Downers Grove, IL: InterVarsity Press, 2006), 3.

6. Ibid., 15–16.

7. Claiborne, 135.

8. Joy Jordan-Lake, *Working Families: Navigating the Demands and Delights of Marriage, Parenting, and Career* (Colorado Springs: WaterBrook Press, 2007), 41.

Chapter 4: The Missional Mom Engages in the Needs of the World

1. Scott Cook, "The Decline of the American Front Porch," http://xroads. virginia.edu/~class/am483_97/projects/cook/decline.htm.

2. David Kirk, "Pleasantville," *New York Times*, September 19, 1999, Books section. www.nytimes.com/books/99/09/19/reviews/990919.19kirplt. html?_r=1

3. Carolyn Custis James, *Lost Women of the Bible* (Grand Rapids, MI: Zondervan, 2005), 36, 44.

4. Jim Wallis, *Rediscovering Values: On Wall Street, Main Street, and Your Street* (New York: Howard Books, 2010), 112.

5. Al Hsu, blog post: http://thesuburbanchristian.blogspot.com/2006/08/global-rich-list-just-how-rich-are-we.html.

6. The photo in reference can be found at http://action.one.org/images/VFphoto_250.png.

7. Alan Hirsch and Debra Hirsch, *Untamed: Reactivating a Missional Form of Discipleship* (Grand Rapids, MI: Baker, 2010), 65. For more on the ministry of Alan and Debra Hirsch, visit their website at www.theforgottenways.org.

8. Shehzad Noorani, "Children of the Black Dust," www.cnn.com/2008/TECH/science/09/28/what.matters.dust/index.html?iref=allsearch.

Chapter 5: The Missional Mom Doesn't "Do Evangelism"

1. This quotation is often attributed to St. Francis of Assisi, although there is no actual source that can confirm this. However, Wendy Murray, author of *A Mended and Broken Heart: The Life and Love of Francis of Assisi* (Basic Books, 1998) says that this "is clearly something he could have said."

2. Portions of this section were adapted from *Growing Healthy Asian American Churches*, edited by Peter Cha, S. Steve Kang, and Helen Lee. © 2006 by Catalyst Leadership Center. Used by permission of InterVarsity Press, P.O. Box 1400, Downers Grove, IL 60515. www.ivpress.com, 123.

3. Brian Simmons, *Falling Away: Why Christians Lose Their Faith & What Can Be Done About It* (Abilene, TX: Hillcrest Publishing Company, 2005).

4. Ken Fong, *Pursuing the Pearl* (Valley Forge, PA: Judson Press, 19990, 104, 114.

5. Quoted from Helen Lee, *Growing Healthy Asian American Churches* (Downers Grove, IL: InterVarsity Press, 2006), 136.

6. Graphic is courtesy of Not Religious, Inc.

7. Alan Hirsch and Debra Hirsch, *Untamed: Reactivating a Missional Form of Discipleship* (Grand Rapids, MI: Baker, 2010), 147.

8. Dave Gibbons, *The Monkey and the Fish* (Grand Rapids, MI: Zondervan, 2009), 116.

9. The Alpha Course is a ten-week experience that many churches use to help people who are curious or interested in the Christian faith learn more in a welcoming, nonthreatening environment. For more information, go to www.alphausa.org.

10. Gibbons, 114, 115.

Chapter 6: The Missional Mom Loves "The Least of These"

1. I'm aware that some feel *The Blind Side* is the Hollywood-ized version of the real story, one that perhaps creates stereotypes of the "white savior" versus the "bad, black mother" as opposed to taking the time to flesh out the characters more thoroughly. Leigh Anne and Sean Tuohy have released their own version of the story, *In a Heartbeat: Sharing the Power of Cheerful Giving* (Henry Holt, 2010). This presents a more balanced picture of all the parties involved, as opposed to reflecting a film director's point of view intended to make a bankable motion picture.

2. Amy Sherman, *Sharing God's Heart for the Poor* (Charlottesville, VA: Trinity Presbyterian Church Urban Ministries, 2000), 22.

3. Arloa Sutter, *The Invisible* (Indianapolis: Wesleyan Publishing House, 2010), 76–77.

4: Ibid.

5. Richard Stearns, *The Hole in Our Gospel* (Nashville: Thomas Nelson, 2009), 22.

6. Wess Stafford, president of Compassion International speaking on Moody Radio's *Midday Connection*, October 9, 2009.

7. Nancy Gibbs, "The Case Against Over-Parenting," *Time*, November 20, 2009.

8. Stearns, 176.

Chapter 7: The Missional Mom Is Third-Culture

1. David Van Biema, "Can Megachurches Bridge the Racial Divide?" *Time*, January 11, 2010.

2. Ibid.

3. Bill Hybels and James Meeks, "Big Questions Our World Must Answer, Part I: Can We Get Along?" Willow Creek Community Church Sermon series, January 19–20, 2008.

4. Dave Gibbons, *The Monkey and the Fish* (Grand Rapids, MI: Zondervan, 2009), 38.

5. Po Bronson and Ashley Merryman, *Nurture Shock* (New York: Hachette Book Group, 2009), 52.

6. Ibid., 55.

Chapter 8: The Missional Mom Creates Missional Families

1. I'd like to express my profound appreciation to the Pearson family for allowing me to share Mary's story and her blog address in this book.

2. Barna Research Group, "Most Twentysomethings Put Christianity on the Shelf Following Spiritually Active Teen Years," September 11, 2006. (www.barna.org/teens-next-gen-articles/147-most-twentysomethings-put-christianity-on-the-shelf-following-spiritually-active-teen-years).

3. Hanna Rosin, "Even Evangelical Teens Do It," *Slate*, May 30, 2007.

4. Ken Fong, "Today's Children Need to Believe That God Is Calling Them to Lead Heroic Lives," blog post, May 2, 2007 (http://sedaqah.xanga.com/588017841/todays-children-need-to-believe-that-god-is-calling-them-to-lead-heroic-lives/).

5. Tracey Bianchi, author of *Green Mama: The Guilt-Free Guide to Helping You and Your Kids Save the Planet* (Zondervan, 2010), also recommends picking up the free pamphlet entitled *Tips for Parenting in a Commercial Culture* and the Wallet Buddy from the Center for the New American Dream, a "thoughtful, proactive organization offering abundant resources for people hoping to make an impact on our consumer-oriented culture" (www. newdream. org/).

6. Julie Clawson's book *Everyday Justice: The Global Impact of our Daily Choices* (InterVarsity Press, 2009) is a helpful and practical book giving guidance on how to make everyday decisions that do not have harmful consequences. Highly recommended.

7. Alan Hirsch and Debra Hirsch, *Untamed: Reactivating a Missional Form of Discipleship* (Grand Rapids, MI: Baker Books, 2010), 172.

8. You can read more about their organization, Karisimbi Business Partners, at www.karisimbipartners.com.

9. Steve Holt, "Idaho's Impact," *Christianity Today*, April 26, 2010.

10. Julie Briggs, blog post: http://roadtoadoption.wordpress.com/2009/02/25/adoption-support-letter/.

11. Colonias exist up and down the Texas side of the border. The word "colonias," which means "neighborhood" in Spanish, resulted when developers bought tracts of farm land and sold them unimproved to mostly poor, Mexican-Americans along the U.S.-Mexico border region. Most colonias people live without basic services taken for granted in the rest of the United States. These unincorporated, isolated settlements often lack water and sewer sys-

tems, electricity, health facilities, paved roads, and safe and sanitary housing. http://www.seco.cpa.state.tx.us/colonias.htm.

Chapter 9: The Missional Mom Is a Culture-Maker

1. There is no way in this limited context that I can do justice to the excellence and depth of thought that is Andy Crouch's *Culture Making*. I encourage all readers to read it in order to better understand how he develops this central premise. Well, well worth the time.

2. Alan Hirsch and Debra Hirsch, *Untamed: Reactivation a Missional Form of Discipleship* (Grand Rapids, MI: Baker Books, 2010), 145.

3. Jennifer Jao, prayer letter. http://www.intervarsity.org/gfm/well/resource/when-blessing-cries.

Chapter 10: The Missional Mom Needs Missional Community

1. Thanks to Eugene Cho, Quest Church, for alerting me to this proverb.

2. This image is not the exact same Wall as at HoneyRock, but it is close. This photo is in the public domain: http://en.wikipedia.org/wiki/File:CCOURSE_LOW_ELEMENTS_010.jpg.

3. Caryn Rivadeneira, *Mama's Got a Fake I.D.* (Colorado Springs: WaterBrook Press, 2009), 69, 70.

4. Krista Petty, "Missional Households" article on Leadership Network website, www.leadnet.org, April 9, 2010. With sincere thanks to Bill White for letting me know about this study.

5. Dave and Jon Ferguson, *Exponential* (Grand Rapids, MI: Zondervan, 2010), 111.

Chapter 11: The Missional Mom Surrenders All

1. Caryn Rivadeneira, *Mama's Got a Fake I.D.* (Colorado Springs: WaterBrook Press, 2009), 179.

2. Heidi Bratton, *Making Peace with Motherhood* (Mahwah, NJ: Paulist Press, 2002), 10–11.

3. Leslie Leyland Fields, "The Myth of the Perfect Parent," *Christianity Today*, January 8, 2010.

4. Keith Meyer is also the author of *Whole Life Transformation: Becoming the Change Your Church Needs* (Downers Grove, IL: InterVarsity Press, 2010).

5. Ed Stetzer and Philip Nation, *Compelled By Love: The Most Excellent Way to Missional Living* (Birmingham: New Hope Publishers, 2008), 32.

6. With gratitude to Arloa Sutter, who alerted me to this benediction.

Bibliography

Ashcroft, Mary Ellen. *Balancing Act: How Women Can Lose Their Roles and Find Their Callings*. Downers Grove, IL: InterVarsity Press, 1996.

Bianchi, Tracey. *Green Mama: The Guilt-Free Guide to Helping You and Your Kids Save the Planet*. Grand Rapids, MI: Zondervan, 2010.

Bramlett, Eric, Dave Ferguson, and Jon Ferguson. *The Big Idea*. Grand Rapids, MI: Zondervan, 2007.

Bratton, Heidi. *Making Peace with Motherhood*. Mahwah, NJ: Paulist Press, 2002.

Bronson, Po, and Ashley Merriman. *Nurture Shock*. New York: Hachette Book Group, 2009.

Brouwer, Douglas. *What Am I Supposed to Do With My Life?* Grand Rapids, MI: Eerdmans Publishing, 2006.

Claiborne, Shane. *Irresistible Revolution*. Grand Rapids, MI: Zondervan, 2006.

Clawson, Julie. *Everyday Justice.* Downers Grove, IL: InterVarsity Press, 2009.

Crouch, Andy. *Culture Making.* Downers Grove, IL: InterVarsity Press, 2008.

Ferguson, Dave, and Jon Ferguson. *Exponential.* Grand Rapids, MI: Zondervan, 2010.

Fields, Leslie Leyland. *Parenting Is Your Highest Calling: And Eight Other Myths That Trap Us In Worry and Guilt.* Colorado Springs: WaterBrook Press, 2008.

Gibbons, Dave. *The Monkey and the Fish.* Grand Rapids, MI: Zondervan, 2009.

Goetz, Dave. *Death by Suburb.* Downers Grove, IL: InterVarsity Press, 2006.

Guinness, Os. *The Call.* Nashville: Word Publishing, 1998.

Heald, Cynthia. *Becoming a Woman of Purpose.* Colorado Springs: NavPress, 2005.

Hirsch, Alan, and Debra Hirsch, *Untamed: Reactivating a Missional Form of Discipleship.* Grand Rapids, MI: Baker, 2010.

James, Carolyn Custis. *Lost Women of the Bible.* Grand Rapids, MI: Zondervan, 2005.

Jordan-Lake, Joy. *Working Families: Navigating the Demands and Delights of Marriage, Parenting, and Career.* Colorado Springs: WaterBrook Press, 2007.

Kristof, Nicholas, and Sheryl WuDunn. *Half the Sky.* New York: Vintage Books, 2009.

Palmer, Parker. *Let Your Life Speak.* Hoboken, NJ: Jossey Bass, 2000.

Rah, Soong-Chan. *The Next Evangelicalism.* Downers Grove, IL: InterVarsity Press, 2009.

Rivadeneira, Caryn. *Mama's Got a Fake I.D.* Colorado Springs: WaterBrook Press, 2009.

Robbins, Alexandra. *The Overachievers: The Secret Lives of Driven Kids.* New York: Hyperion, 2006.

Sherman, Amy. *Sharing God's Heart for the Poor.* Charlottesville, NC: Trinity Presbyterian Church Urban Ministries, 2000.

Stearns, Richard. *The Hole in Our Gospel.* Nashville: Thomas Nelson, 2009.

Stetzer, Ed, and Philip Nation. *Compelled by Love.* Birmingham, AL: New Hope Publishers, 2008.

Wallis, Jim. *Rediscovering Values: On Wall Street, Main Street and Your Street.* New York: Howard Books, 2010.

Young, Ed. *Kid CEO.* Nashville: Faith Words, 2004.

Acknowledgments

If I could, I would put many more names on the cover of this book than just my own. I now appreciate the communal effort behind every book I've ever read.

Steve Lyon, Deborah Keiser, Holly Kisly, Carolyn McDaniel, and the rest of the Moody team—thank you for believing in this project. It's been a dream process! Annette LaPlaca, I'm so grateful for your partnership in editing and your words of encouragement.

Chris Park, you are an agent extraordinaire and a missional mom if I ever met one. Here's to many more projects together!

I'm grateful to Carla Barnhill and Caryn Rivadeneira, who have been on this journey with me since its earliest stage. To the amazing Redbud Writers Guild (www.redbudwritersguild.com)—thank you for your encouragement and for reading countless revisions. Angie, Anita, Arloa, Caryn, Jen, Karen, Keri, Melinda, Princess, Shayne, Suanne, Tracey: here's to the power of words to make a difference in the world!

Marshall Shelley and Skye Jethani, this book would not exist if you hadn't first given me the chance to write about the missional church. Thank you!

Regina and Madison Trammel, thank you both for supporting the early conceptions of this project and helping it get to the next level. Wendy Murray, you rescued me with your insightful comments and direction. Jenn Hua, you're as good an editor as you are a friend! Ed Gilbreath, your encouragement kept me afloat. Bill and Katy White, you were such a wealth of knowledge, experience, information, inspiration, and connections! You made me want to move to Paramount. Phil Pearson, thanks for being such a great role model to our boys and giving me time to write! Joe and Esther Liaw, Eddie and Kristen Yoon, and Pastor Peter Park: thanks for your friendship, support, and for reading drafts!

As I was unable to quote every wise and wonderful word from those I interviewed, I'd like to recognize these amazing missional moms: Susan Arico, Shelley Bacote, Amy Julia Becker, Melinda Boyle, Julie Briggs, Nadene Brunk, Kafi Carrasco, Patsy Chavarria, Minhee Cho, Catherine Crouch, Sue Ferguson, Rae Ann Fitch, Dana Gilbreath, Laura Goetsch, Jennifer Grant, Tonya Herman, Carisa Hinson, Cyd Holsclaw, Mae Hong, Jennifer Jao, Jennifer Jukanovich, Esther Lee, Betty Marmolejo, Frederica Mathewes-Green, Scottie May, Shayne Moore, Elisa Morgan, Marta Newkirk, Diane Padilla, Stacy Paolella, Josie Schopen, Grace Shim, Amy Simpson, Kirsten Strand, Arloa Sutter, Kathy Tuan-MacLean, Diane Uy, Rachel VerWys, Katy White, and Mayling Wong-Squires. Your lives inspire me to missional living!

To the extended Lee family, thank you for prayers, emotional support, and especially for watching over my kids when I was in solitary confinement! I am ever grateful for each of you.

Last but most definitely not least, my amazing husband, Brian, sacrificed summers and vacations and countless Fridays to give me precious time, in addition to reading the book and offering great suggestions and encouragement. I can't thank you enough. My three boys, Jason, Sean, and Aidan—thanks for so many prayers for Mom! I love seeing how God is growing in your hearts every day.

I serve and love a God of immeasurable grace and mercy, and if this book has touched you in any way, it is all due to Him and all for His glory. Amen!

HELEN LEE

Helen Lee is an award-winning Christian journalist who has worked and written for numerous periodicals such as *Christianity Today, Leadership Journal, Today's Christian Woman*, and *re:generation quarterly*. She lives in Chicagoland with her husband and three boys, whom she homeschools using a classical Christian approach. Helen is a proud member of the Redbud Writers Guild, a group that seeks to help women find their voice in order to transform the world. She welcomes your comments and feedback about *The Missional Mom*; please visit HelenLee.info.

MOODY
PUBLISHERS

moodypublishers.com

REAL MOMS ... REAL JESUS

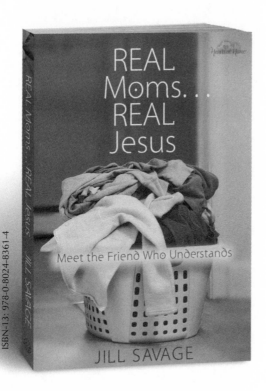

What does Jesus know about the peanut-butter-and-jelly life of a mom? Plenty! Jill Savage, founder and director of Hearts at Home, introduces the real Jesus to real moms. In chapters that examine key behaviors and decisions Jesus made during His life on earth, Jill brings those lessons right down to the laundry-filled, sticky-fingered days every mother knows.

MOODY
PUBLISHERS

moodypublishers.com

GROWING GRATEFUL KIDS

Even when economic times are tight, our children enjoy an abundance of material possessions. Yet, amidst all this wealth, discontentment and competition seem to be on the rise. With the currents of materialism and entitlement flowing so strong, how do we raise kids who are simply thankful? With simple language, interesting anecdotes, and biblical applications, Susie Larson helps readers understand that although teaching perspective and gratitude to our children is critical, it is not difficult.

MOODY
PUBLISHERS

moodypublishers.com